MW00576132

Praise for the Society of Classical Poets (SCP)

"The SCP is a tremendously important and vital organ of the poetry world, and one that seems to be growing. I hope it will retain the fine mix that it has now of mature work, amateur work, and the work of novices and students. This makes the SCP profoundly democratic, and also an excellent teaching tool. I also think that the unfettered nature of the discourse at the SCP now stands quite alone in the world of online poetry venues."

> —Dr. Joseph S. Salemi, TRINACRIA Editor, Professor, New York University, Hunter College

"SCP is a vital fortress against those who tear down all we have inherited across Western civilization. Our ancestors fought on, and so must we."

> —Michael Charles Maibach, Managing Director, James Wilson Institute

"The world is better for the Society of Classical Poets, poets are better by comradery and competition, and I am heartened that we might rebuild a new Beauty on the old Foundation."

> —Michael Curtis, Sculptor, Architect, Poet, and Author

"[The SCP] has a magnanimous stance, marvelous breadth of content relevant to contemporary life, and has responsibly brought traditional values of life, art, and poetic form forward into the daylight, and put the idea of deity back into poetry in the modern era."

> —Damian Robin, Writer and Editor, *The Epoch Times*

"Thank you very much for helping to keep traditional verse alive—it is appreciated more widely than you may know!"

—a Long Island, New York poet

"After years of trying to shoehorn my rhyming poetry into so-called 'open' publications I have become convinced that there is no outlet for such verse, so I'm very happy to have stumbled across your site. Initially as a poet I assumed that like everyone else I would write free verse but more and more my work resolved into classical forms, especially sonnets which I believe to be shamefully disparaged in our age."

—a UK poet

"Even if you choose not to accept this, I just wanted to say thank you for having a 'Society' like this! I've been getting pretty sick and tired of all the poetry websites/magazines that only feature 'free verse'! The Society of the Classical Poets is like a breath of fresh air to me, so thank you!"

—an award-winning high school poet

"Incidentally, I want to make one thing clear: I am a Catholic, and I support Christian America. It was refreshing to discover a non-anti-Christian literary organization in operation. Thank you everyone at the Society for defending real poetry."

—a Japanese poet

THE SOCIETY OF
CLASSICAL POETS

JOURNAL XI

Mantyk · Anderson · Grein · Magdalen

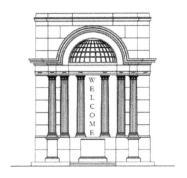

Classical Poets Publishing

———————

Mount Hope, New York

Editors: Evan Mantyk (Lead), C.B. Anderson
(General Editing), Dusty Grein (Layout), Daniel Magdalen (Art)

All poems granted permission by poets and previously published on the Society of
Classical Poets' website ClassicalPoets.org between February 1, 2022, and
January 31, 2023

All contemporary artwork used with permission of the artist. Other artwork are in the
public domain.

Cover Art Front: *Shakespeare* by Gary Lee Price

Cover Art Back: *Brightness of Night* by Xiaoping Chen

"The Society of Classical Poets Edifice" on title page by Michael Curtis

Inquiries and Membership: submissions@classicalpoets.org

ISBN: 978-1-949398-78-6

Contents

INTRODUCTION

For those new to the Society of Classical Poets, this printed journal you now hold is a selection of poetry and essays from the Society's website, which acts as an ongoing online journal of poetry, and to a lesser extent of essays, art, and music. This publication is limited to poetry and essays published by the Society between February 1, 2022 and January 31, 2023, and is not intended to include previously published work. Art is specially selected for this journal with an emphasis on featuring the works of living artists, not necessarily to perfectly match poems, which is different from the Society's website where art is intended to match poems.

The poetry published by the Society of Classical Poets pays close attention to meter as the basic requirement. With the exception of the syllable-counting used to write a haiku and the purposely doggerel-like clerihew, all of the poetry contained herein has a discernible meter, following in the footsteps of Homer, Virgil, Dante Alighieri, William Shakespeare, John Milton, Henry Longfellow, Edgar Allan Poe, Robert Frost, and many many others. Consistent meter is the foundational technique in terms of the language itself. Rhyme, alliteration, and other techniques follow on top of that foundation. The meter creates a sense of music, and one might say enchantment, from the very first words onward.

What is important and what I have to frequently tell people is that counting syllables is not meter. A line of iambic pentameter does not always have 10 syllables. So if you can't hear the unstressed-stressed unit of meter, then there is no point in composing a 100-line poem and submitting it. You are much better off working on a four-line poem in perfect iambic tetrameter.

Now that I've mentioned "perfect meter" though, I should mention that there is another group of poets (recovering from the bad acid trip of solipsistic free verse I suspect) who cling to extreme formal verse that always has perfect meter. To those counting ten syllables and to those professing the virtues of perfect meter all of the time, I've said the same thing so often that I might as well put it here: The most famous line of iambic pentameter is Shakespeare's "to BE or NOT to BE that IS the QUEStion," which is 11 syllables because of that extra unstressed beat ("-tion") at the end. Writing in iambic pentameter simply means you will have five stressed beats by the end of the line and they will tend to (but not always) occur in an iambic pattern. The total number of syllables will not always be 10. If you are an aspiring poet and can't hear the meter yet, then you should just focus on hearing it. High school students, in particular, who are forced to write a poem should have the option to count syllables if they can't hear the meter. If you can hear the meter and you still want not a single extra unstressed beat in there—and perhaps would wag your finger even at Shakespeare's "To be or not to be" line—then chances are that the more poetry you write or publish in absolutely perfect meter, the more unnatural and awkward it will sound. You will be putting too much emphasis on the surface-level technique and not enough on the meaning and narrative flow of the poem.

Meter, rhyme, and so on are part of the language itself. But that is only part of poetry, not the whole experience. The meaning and storytelling of a poem are grounded in the handling of metaphor, personification, idioms, and so on. Last year, the poet James A. Tweedie created his own definition of formal (or classical) poetry and left it open for comment:

> The working of magic with words, rhythm, rhyme and form to conjure, spin, and weave an image, a story, a feeling, an idea, in such a way that it comes alive in the reader's mind as vividly and indelibly as possible.

While no definition could probably be perfect, Mr. Tweedie has made an admirable attempt here that I think is instructive. He pulls together the two main elements I am referring to, the language ("words, rhythm, rhyme and form") and meaning ("an image, a story, a feeling, an idea"). These are two elements that must be worked at, and part of that working is balancing their demands.

New readers should also note: you certainly may not agree with all of the opinions expressed in the poems and essays in this book. That is perfectly fine. I do not agree with them all either, and I'm the editor! For example, as you will read in his essay, Dr. Salemi finds it untenable that Shakespeare's plays may not have been written by the man named

William Shakespeare. However, I personally find the Earl of Oxford theory quite compelling. We disagree… so what? I put forward in a poem that Darwinian evolution is false, and that believing in God should mean that you do not believe in Darwinian evolution. You may disagree, but again so what? This journal is about poetry first and foremost and not about individual perspectives. No poems or essays contained herein represent some kind of official view of the Society of Classical Poets, which is simply a group of poets dedicated to the flourishing of traditional verse. It is just that poets are people and people have perspectives and those are reflected in their poetry. Anyone of any faith can enjoy the religious music of Johann Sebastian Bach and the religious art of Leonardo da Vinci. So too can anyone enjoy this journal.

Yet we live in an age where people are being attacked and deplatformed merely for their views. Just this last year, the Society of Classical Poets was deplatformed by Winning Writers, who said it was because of "posts mocking the transgender community and expressing support for fascist-adjacent politicians like Giorgia [sic] Meloni." (Giorgi Meloni is the current prime minister of Italy and is pretty centrist, and Dr. Salemi wrote a poem in her praise that I had published.) On its About page, the news website Whatfinger has a pretty striking clarification that speaks well to this trend. The people who run Whatfinger are military veterans who may not be as eloquent as the poets featured in this journal, but they have perfectly spoken to this issue in plain language, regarding their own website, and I think we could apply it just as well to this journal:

> Honest…if you are a 'snowflake' in any way, you might have a heart attack and die from what you will find here on both ends of the spectrum. We do not believe in censorship here, and we do not believe in the fake speech codes of the politically correct. Our Bill of Rights DOES NOT have a clause for 'hate speech'. There is no such thing as hate speech and if you believe there is, then you have no clue as to why the Constitution of the United States was written as it was. If there is any speech that needs to be protected, guess what? It is what you consider to be 'hate speech'. So put your big boy or big girl pants on, man up and be prepared to learn more…

Thank you, Whatfinger, for your effective wit and for linking to many of our poems online.

Finally, for those returning to this Journal, note that we have continued to reduce the number of chapters, amalgamating three more chapters in the first chapter The Muse's Song and the third chapter, renamed Light Verse and Satire. The idea behind these changes is to create a more varied and enjoyable reading experience. Your feedback is always welcome.

—Evan Mantyk, March 2023

I. THE MUSE'S SONG

Ode to Winter

by Susan Jarvis Bryant

A honeypool of sun seeps from the skies.
The crisp and clingy leaves have lost their grip.
   My scarlet spirits dip
As gold and russet highs bid cold goodbyes.
I feel your icy bite in twilight's breeze—
   Your stinging chill;
Your silver nip; your hoary, moon-licked tease
That bends the naked branches to your will.

You suck the thrumming blood from Gaia's veins,
Then frost her plump and sumptuous autumn spill—
   That juicy-berry fill
For scrawny critters scouring country lanes.
You scythe through field and fen through thick of night.
   A rush of breath
Drifts from your lips to fog the spangled light
Where reapers creep and mortals peek at death.

Your presence comes with promise to excite
With dreamy scenes of lacy flakes of snow.
   You leave blue souls aglow
With memories of Christmases of white—
Your shining shawl of glory swathing earth
   As sleigh bells ring.
I know your rage and grace. I know your worth.
I know your savage splendor gift-wraps Spring.

The Wind

by Martin Rizley

Listen, listen! Do you hear it? It is on the march tonight—
The incessant winter wind that blows throughout the wood and glade.
Like a spectral army passing through the night in grim parade—
Do you hear its restless movement where no moonbeam sheds it light?
Do you hear the countless legions as they march both far and near
In the shade of gloomy bowers and across the open lea,
Through the waves of high grass rolling like a tempest troubled sea—
Do you hear their footfalls echo in the wild atmosphere?

Do you hear their creaking wagons rumble down the darkened lane,
And their ghostly drummers beating out a melancholy dirge?
Do you hear from time to time an eerie moaning sound emerge
As their weary voices join to sing a wordless song of pain?

In the gusts that keep on blowing, do you hear their riders charge
On the backs of phantom horses through the tops of twisting trees?
Under angry anvil skies they fly, as if to chase the breeze,
Leaping ledges, trampling hedges, as they tear along at large.

Through the night they keep on racing where no human eye can see,
Blazing trails through tangled forests, dashing down the inky stream,
Speeding forward, fast, and fearsome, yet as a fleeting as a dream,
As they gallop ever onward in their ghostly company.

Like the souls of fallen soldiers trudging homeward, battle worn,
Unaware the war is over, and the victory is lost,
Do you hear them shuffle past you in the woods by winter tossed
In their slow and sad retreat before the bright brigade of morn?

In Winter Some Find Beauty

by Carl Kinsky

Just stubble's left where once stalks stood in rows.
Where tassels rustled during summer rains,
snow's scattered like salt spread so nothing grows
Except for loneliness and empty pain.

Above in meadows where lean calves grew fat,
abundance gently reigned and creatures teemed;
now grasses cower, safer to lay flat
and silent while winds tear and ravens scream.

On hilltops stand trees, shivering, beseeching
the heavens, beggars pleading with the sky
for warmth, more daylight, leafless branches reaching
for answers but receiving no reply.

In winter some find beauty though it be
A beauty for eyes blind to what I see.

Yet

by James A. Tweedie

The withered dune grass slumps beneath a sere
Gray frozen sky, as winter tag-teams fall
And nighttime frost compels the Black-Tailed deer
To seek out warmer lairs beneath the tall,

Cone-laden Sitka spruce. The screech of jays
Intone a requiem for summers past,
And fading memories of once-lived days
Grieve "might-have-beens" that long-since breathed their last.

As chill-red sunsets summon forth the stars
And darkness shrouds a world entombed by night,
With lidless eyes we carry unhealed scars
Of broken dreams and wrongs not yet made right.

Yet each new dawn, a-bloom with lightful hours,
Will bear the scent of spring, new hope, and flowers.

Original French

Le temps a laissié son manteau
De vent, de froidure, et de pluye,
Et s'est vestu de brouderie
De soleil luyant, cler et beau.

Il n'y a beste, ne oyseau,
Qu'en son jargon chante ou crie
Le temps [a laissié son manteau.]

Riviere, fontaine, et ruisseau
Portent, en livree jolie,
Gouttes d'argent d'orfaverie;
Chascun s'abille de nouveau
Le temps [a laissié son manteau.]

The Spring

by Charles d'Orléans (1394–1465)
translated by Margaret Coats

The Spring has left off Winter's cloak
Of wind and rain and frosty sting;
She's dressed in broidered blanketing
Of beauties sunlight can evoke.

The beasts and birds, wild forest folk,
All roar and chirp and croak and sing
   The Spring.

The rivers, brooks, and fountains soak
The earth with silver drops, and fling
Pied jewels throughout fields blossoming.
All things vest new, and freshly yoke
   The Spring.

17

Proserpine by Nicolàs Fasolino, 2022, oil on linen, 29 1/2 x 17 1/2 in.,
Art Renewal Center Collection. (Instagram.com/nico_fasolino)

May Day

Maypoles were a feature of ancient Roman festivals to mark the renewal of Spring. The feast days of Saints Philip and James were celebrated by the Church of England in May.

by Cheryl Corey

Having hewed a length of pine,
   They drove it in the ground;
Then word was spread throughout the town,
   "Ye comers gather round.

Now let us make a joyful song
   And share with all good cheer;
The stage is set, the men have brewed
   Ten barrelsful of beer."

And so began the merriment,
   Commencing with the drum,
A cannon shot, a round of fire,
   And instruments to strum.

They took the streamers in their hands
   And danced around the pole;
They sang in praise of saints who died
   To save the mortal soul.

They feasted well, and all the day
   Was full of heady mirth;
To see the goddess Maia bring
   The seasonal rebirth.

Original Middle English

Whan that Aprill with his shoures soote
The droghte of March hath perced to the roote,
And bathed every veyne in swich licour
Of which vertu engendred is the flour;
Whan Zephirus eek with his sweete breeth
Inspired hath in every holt and heeth
The tendre croppes, and the yonge sonne
Hath in the Ram his half cours yronne,
And smale foweles maken melodye,
That slepen al the nyght with open ye
(So priketh hem Nature in hir corages),
Thanne longen folk to goon on pilgrimages,
And palmeres for to seken straunge strondes,
To ferne halwes, kowthe in sondry londes;
And specially from every shires ende
Of Engelond to Caunterbury they wende,
The hooly blisful martir for to seke,
That hem hath holpen whan that they were seeke.

The Canterbury Tales—General Prologue

Lines 1-18

by Geoffrey Chaucer (1343-1400)
translated by Evan Mantyk

When April's sweetest showers downward shoot,
The drought of March is pierced right to the root
Through every vein with liquid of such power
And virtue that it generates the flower;
When Zephyrus too exhales his breath so sweet
Inspiring in ground beneath the feet
The tender crops, and there's a youthful sun,
His second half course through the Ram now run,
And little birds start making melodies
Who sleep all night eyes open in the trees
(For Nature pricks them in each little heart),
On pilgrimage then folks desire to start.
The palmers seek to make their travel plans
For far-off shrines renowned in sundry lands.
Especially from every English town
To Canterbury now their steps are bound,
To seek the holy blissful martyr quick
Who helped them out when once they had been sick.

The Recollected Dream

by David Watt

When midsummer rain is spearing
From storm clouds darkest grey
That provide no hint of clearing
To reveal the blue of day,
The scent from marshland grasses
Permeates each breath of air
That summons as it passes,
Winged creatures from their lair.

Then the wattled spur-winged plovers,
In their element at last,
Re-emerge from reedy covers,
Seeking out a worm repast—
And the droplets from their wattles
Drip on sheath and blade below,
And the soil horizon mottles
Where the trickling waters flow.

Soon the plovers start their calling
That more often graces night,
And the haunting notes keep falling
On a landscape spare of light
Until the torrent ceases,
Re-admitting hidden rays—
And though the spell releases,
The ghostly memory stays.

Now I wait till warm days brew it—
A thunderous downfall,
To renew the did-he-do-it
Of the plover's plaintive call,
Carried clear and unaffected
Though the waters fairly teem,
Proving that calls recollected
Hadn't risen from a dream.

Spirit-bird by Herman Smorenburg, 2008, oil on panel, 23.6 x 19.6 in. (Hermansmorenburg.com)

Elysium

by Adam Sedia

O golden hour, soft denouement of day,
O mystic time of quietude and peace,
When boughs and rushes whisper as they sway,
Twirled by the sighing zephyrs' soft caprice;

When, fallen from his blinding noonday height,
The dimmed, declining sun, departing west,
Immerses all in glowing, golden light—
Warm relict of the noon's blaze that oppressed.

When all the din and tumult day has stirred
Recedes to silence, hushed beneath the breeze,
And only owl and nightingale are heard
Calling out gently from the rustling trees;

You wearied soul, who now seek only rest
At daytime's end, bask in the golden gleam,
The stillness, the mild airs, this world caressed
In light and languor, glimpsed as in a dream—

Your refuge, this imprint on earthly soil
Of fields beyond the sunset, ever green,
Where blessed spirits know no care nor toil,
Eternally at peace in such a scene.

But this, its mortal counterpart, flies back
Beyond the skies, now leaving them to turn
To evening's pink, then twilight's blue, then black
Of night, whose distant lights but faintly burn.

Ever Flowing

by Dusty Grein

Upon the rushing river's bank I stand,
deep water, ever flowing as it goes.
The turbulence of my life it reflects
as if my mortal pain, it truly knows.

I close my eyes while cruel heartache builds
and boils. It swirls and churns from deep within,
akin to eddies in the river's course,
all ever flowing seaward as they spin.

A lifetime lived within each second's tick,
my heart's emotions ever flowing strong
form rapids, waterfalls, and twisting turns,
which carve deep channels as they sing love's song.

Though time often appears to stand quite still,
it's always ever flowing, moving fast;
toward blank tomorrows and the great unknown,
each day it takes us further from the past.

Through waves of dappled light and shadows dark
we chart the river's course each day anew,
as yearning, ever flowing, on we roll,
to seek the distant rest of oceans, blue.

Before us lies the fear of change and loss—
deep love becomes deep grief when torn apart.
Time's ever flowing nature is our bane,
yet passing time can mend a broken heart.

My life's become the river's equal now,
surviving ever flowing pain and grief
while drawing strength from pools of love and faith,
I cherish moments calm, however brief.

For Love of the Sea

by Catherine Lee

Thalassa spoke when as a child I played upon the sand—
her swirling foam a gentle whisper I could understand.
In playful mood I'd chase her just to run from her in glee,
then stop—allow my feet to be caressed by teasing sea.
She spoke with enigmatic sighs of lands so far away—
I'd sit and listen, lick my face of salty windblown spray.

She called to me throughout the years, beguiled me with her charm
and mesmerized, delighted me—her beauty could disarm.
She summoned me persistently; I missed her when away—
her therapeutic greatness, her spectacular display.
Enchanted, captured by her spell I'd stroll along the shore
admiring her magnificence till I could walk no more.

I've sailed upon her surface, gazed in staggered disbelief
when plunging into chambers deep to view her coral reef,
cocooned in silence all around in Triton's hidden world
to marvel at the multicolored splendor there unfurled.
I've surfed her splendid pipelines, felt momentum unsurpassed,
and stolen countless fish from her with all the lines I've cast.

She beckoned in the evenings with her sensuality,
the moon's reflection on her face creating mystery,
her quietness inscrutable, yet hushed seductive tones
would hold me captivated, sending shivers through my bones.
Her Sirens on those balmy nights intoxicated me—
she stole my heart forever, this alluring, regal sea.

I've seen her calm and tranquil lying blissfully serene,
providing yachts with refuge moored in harbors safe, pristine
whilst white-winged birds shrieked loudly as they hovered in the sky,
admired a pod of dolphins as they've swiftly coasted by,
surveyed the dancing whitecaps when the summer breezes blow
and sunlight glistening brightly on his looking glass below.

I've heard Poseidon bellow and observed with anxious awe
as fearsome forces gathered, rose to crash upon the shore
with raging waters pounding, power nothing can withstand,
as if to prove their mastery of this primeval land—
her impact carving mountains over every century
to sculpt dramatic cliffs, create the coastline of the sea.

Her many moods astound me. She is beautiful and still,
yet treacherous and unforgiving, wild and cruel at will.
I've envied her unleashed emotions passionate and raw,
her silence, freedom, solitude, potential to restore,
respected her invincible and vast supremacy,
secure within her might and her assumed infinity.

So at my end when nothing's left my solitude to ease,
I pray Thalassa calls me still with precious memories.
As long as I can watch her endless steadfast roll and surge,
the sight will take away my pain and all misgivings purge.
Then happily I'll listen to that constant ebb and flow,
which drew me as a child and gripped my spirit long ago.

I know her soothing presence will surround me with her peace.
I'll happily surrender to her lure of sweet release.
One final time she'll speak to me, her voice will fill my mind
and gladly I will ride that swell and never look behind.
I'll close my eyes and drop my weary head upon my chest—
the sea will fill my heart and soul and carry me to rest.

THALASSA: Greek goddess of the Sea

Jason and the Argo by Eric Armusik, 2019, oil on birch, 20 x 16 in. (Ericarmusik.com)

Valiant Men

by Angel L. Villanueva

The sailors brave the angry storm
   As waves the ocean brings.
It seems to them one hundred years
Of fighting death despite their fears,
   Like ancient warring kings.

The frigid water stings their hands
   And chills their sodden skin.
But they confront the ghastly howls
And fight with death as thunder growls,
   To reach their land and kin.

The valiant men unite as one
   And bravely surge ahead.
No wave, or grave, their will can break
Nor dim the morning light to wake;
   They fight for life instead.

But there, behind a swelling wave,
   A larger one, they see.
And so they pray their ship holds out
As they again attempt to rout
   A sanguinary sea.

Deschutes River Reverie

by James A. Tweedie

The river, swift and shallow, roils its way
Beneath the outstretched arms of old-growth pines,
Past bank-side willows diamond-dewed with spray,
And hillside ferns and thimbleberry vines.

A fallen cedar, once a forest lord,
Contributes to the nascent euphony
As broken branches add a vocal chord
To water-music's choral symphony.

Behind the cedar lies a quiet spot
Where wrist-flicked Pregnant Adams gently lands.
With flash and tug, a German Brown is caught
And gently held in two well-moistened hands.

The barbless hook removed, the trout set free,
An Upper Deschutes River reverie.

PREGNANT ADAMS: an artificial dry fly used in fly fishing.

Dark Sky

by Joseph Stuart

Back home, the dark is overborne
By a billion busy diodes
Emitting artificial light,
Thence seeping out into the night.

But, up here, there are auroras,
Constellations, and nebulae—
Or so the motel owners say:
"Last week, we saw the Milky Way."

So, we wind through wooded headlands
To join a remnant, dousing lamps,
Spraying mists of citronella,
Lying down and looking stellar.

Like unto ancients gazing up
To see a billion burning fires
Ages past—a cloud of witness
Now revealed, but just in darkness.

Original French

Les cieux resplendissant d'Étoiles
Aux radieux frissonnements
Ressemblent à des flots dormants
Que sillonnent de blanches voiles.

Quand l'azur déchire ses voiles,
Nous voyons les bleus firmaments,
Les cieux resplendissant d'Étoiles
Aux radieux frissonnements.

Quel peintre mettra sur ses toiles,
O Dieu, ces clairs fourmillements,
Ces fournaises de diamants
Qu'à mes yeux ravis tu dévoiles,
Les cieux resplendissant d'Étoiles.

The Stars

by Théodore de Banville (1823-1891)
translated by Margaret Coats

The heavens glittering with stars
In frosty brilliance shimmering
Resemble billows slumbering
With white caps under sails and spars.

When day pulls azure veils toward bars,
We see the dark sky flickering,
The heavens glittering with stars
In frosty brilliance shimmering.

What painter could with peerless arts,
O God, show sparkles glimmering
From diamond bonfires simmering
That to my ravished eyes you bring,
The heavens glittering with stars!

The Stonechat Listens at the Asylum Window

Stonechat: a type of small bird

by Charles Southerland

I fear I might mistranslate what you said
And lose the very essence of your words.
May I record you as I do the birds:
The warbler, shrike and wren, red's wild-combed head
Who can't fly straight because his wings are strained
By his erratic breaths—the young cock quail
Who only knows four notes, the nightingale?
Perhaps the mockingbird who has profaned
The puerile bluebird to his detriment?
I listen to them all here in the field
Or from the house, the wood, the swimming pond,
The deer-stand in the right-of-way, the tent
I hid in, hunting, while my body healed—
As you well know, from wreckage and its rent.
You are the bird of paradise; I'm fond
Of you beyond compare, despite your squawk
When you were ill with me, the bedroom talk,
Too colorful for feathers to respond.
But when you left, it was the hardest thing,
This separation. Distance has allure,
It surely does. Migration's not a cure.
These days, your speech has turned to twittering.
I asked if you were lonely; you said, no.
I wondered if I heard you nearly right.
I am the red-winged blackbird's gulping tone,
The swallow, swift, the collared dove, hoopoe—
No, not the Merlin, hunting late tonight.
I am the loon, I am the loon, alone.

Landscape at Dawn (霧曉圖) by Xiaoping Chen, 1990, watercolor on rice paper, 16x30 in.

Haiku

The following above haiku include the winner and some of the runners-up in the Society of Classical Poets 2022 Haiku Competition, Judged by Margaret Coats

a cicada's husk
grandfather in his best suit
hands folded, eyes closed

  —Ngo Binh Anh Khoa

The night condenses
into black brown coffee drops.
They stain the morning.

  —Ezeifedi Chibueze

New blooms on black trees
veiled in quiet bone-white fog
spring's dirge to winter

  —Hannah Lee

high-rise balcony
the perfect panorama
of summertime smog

    —Srini

Fall's artillery
Acorns spatter on my roof
Rat! Tat! Winter comes

    —John Sheills

lost in perfumed air
a small skipper is crossing
the wildflower sea

    —Benjamin Bläsi

a hot summer night
only a slice of the moon
for my refreshment

    —Urszula Marciniak

What Geese May Teach

by Sally Cook

My mother had the power that knowledge wields,
So questions such as—*Would you like to go?*
Were never invitations, but commands
To fly away, cross yellow fields and low,
Like summer insects, stuck upon windshields.
A raggle-taggle group we were, and so
Like sandflies could not change what time demands.

Beneath a half-known psychic undertow,
My mother screeched her well-worn, wearing wheels
As we pulled up to watch the wild geese soar
In ordered honking triangles. Much more,
We'd missed such ordered symmetry before.

The Cricket

by Jeffrey Essmann

These mornings there's a cricket cross the way
Whose chirrup purls and eddies in the air,
Autumnal now and cool, to counterpoint
The city's muffled thrum as well anoint
The drowsy traipsing of my early prayer.

A cricket on the hearth is luck, it's said,
And though to call an empty New York lot
A hearth may be a metaphor too far,
The thought of luck itself is quite bizarre,
And either one buys into it or not.

In general I trust grace far more than luck,
Yet looking at the world and its upsets,
Although I know full well I should have qualms
At mixing lucky crickets with my psalms,
There's mornings I must cover all my bets.

Looking Them Over by Tim Cox, 2020, oil on canvas, 18 x 24 in.,
cropped image. (Timcox.com)

41

Toward Yehuling, 1211

The battle at Yehuling (literally "Wild Fox Ridge") was the first major struggle between the Jin Dynasty and the increasingly-powerful Mongol Empire. The march toward Yehuling began in the early spring of 1211. The Mongol victory there would culminate 23 years later in the collapse of the Jin Dynasty.

by Talbot Hook

Unfolding steppes emerge as flattened plains
Of long grasses of gold and April-green,
While crystal streams, like bold and careless children,
Careen away through boundless fallow fields.

Horses graze nearby on budding sprouts
While courtly falcon streaks the sky alone,
Now mantled in the palest morning sun—
As all of under-heaven slowly thaws.

The squatting yurts that stud the overcast
Horizon offer up their steles of smoke.
The men astride their horses test the air,
Descrying signs in wind and warming soil.

    For soon it will be time.
    Soon hooves will faintly stir
    From sleep a bounded land
    And whisper words of war.

Across the plains, beyond the sleep-eyed herd,
A snaking wall of stone, a coiled shield:
A hoary dragon sinews mountain paths
With flame enough for countless men and steeds.

But here the pasture plains are yet untrammeled;
Here the runnels course like wayward foals.
Here fires only warm, and bowmen hunt,
And here still flows the milk of paradise.

The Agony and The Ecstasy

by Gail Kaye Naegele

I beg among the lonely hours
  oblivious to time and space
and pace beneath the Sistine towers
  where pigments paint my puzzled face.
Why call me to divine commission,
as if I am the King's magician,
to turn blank skies to holy vision;
  oblivious to time and space?

I flee to hills of alabaster,
  where ancient gods sleep in soft stone;
there gaze at dawn from fields of aster,
  in sunlit clouds, behold a throne!
Benign, God glows in grace and glory,
his finger tracing allegory,
on clear blue skies creation's story
  His vision of the towers shone.

With passion's pulse I paint the towers
  as form and color mold blank sky;
a tempest tethered endless hours
  to paint the vision or to die.
Though my flesh and bones are aching,
for beauty's cause the world forsaking,
for splendor by His love creating
  and as I paint I sing and cry.

NOTE: Selected from the Classic Movie-Inspired Poem Challenge initiated by
Susan Jarvis Bryant

43

Original Spanish

Desde la Torre

Retirado en la paz de estos desiertos,
Con pocos, pero doctos libros juntos,
Vivo en conversación con los difuntos,
Y escucho con mis ojos a los muertos.

Si no siempre entendidos, siempre abiertos,
O enmiendan, o fecundan mis asuntos;
Y en músicos callados contrapuntos
Al sueño de la vida hablan despiertos.

Las Grandes Almas que la Muerte ausenta,
De injurias de los años vengadora,
Libra, ¡oh gran Don Josef!, docta la Imprenta.

En fuga irrevocable huye la hora;
Pero aquélla el mejor cálculo cuenta,
Que en la lección y estudios nos mejora.

From the Tower

by Francisco de Quevedo (1580-1645)
translated by Elwin Wirkala

Retired to these deserts and at peace,
and with but few, though learnèd, books beside,
I live conversing now with the deceased,
and listen with my eyes to those who died.

Open, whether or not I miss their points,
they mend or fecundate my everything,
their music's muted counterpoints when joined
with this life's dream bespeak awakening.

Great Souls absented by mortality,
in death avenging injuries of years,
the learnèd press, Oh Josef, has set free!

Hours fled forever disappear,
but they are best accounted for in letters,
read and studied, when they make us better.

Sumo's Winning Ways

by Margaret Coats

Fierce frontal impact clenches victory
In less time than an untrained eye can blink,
But connoisseurs of sumo's treasury
Prefer discriminating knack. They wink
When force through fine technique shows mastery.

Drive into the opponent, pull him close,
Then push him, force him, thrust him, crush him out,
Or pull or slap him down to hard-packed dirt.
Twist, pivot, lock his arm or head—and throw!

Throw with authority, because the aim
Is winning! Seconds in the ring repay
The hours and years spent training. Not a game
Is this; give everything you've got to sway
The foe off balance, and your triumph claim.

Throw overarm or underarm or hip;
Use leg trips or a hammer body drop,
A double leg sweep or a hooking twist,
Or all your strength to lift him out—take risks.

The thrill of winning stormy breakneck bouts
By spirit and technique, the fighter's pride,
Deserves his effort and the viewers' shouts;
His body's massive learning can decide
Contentions won through sudden whirlabouts.

To size and strength and speed and skill, add stealth.
Surprises win: a dodge or jump or block;
Clap hands in the rival's face, or slap it hard;
An ankle pick can do the cheeky trick.

New moves that foreign wrestlers introduce,
Reviving clever clashes of the past,
Shock all who let them fall into disuse.
Be quick to study; make a counterblast
Bold, common, unexpected, or abstruse:

The backward belt toss, pulling body slam,
Rear lean out, grabbing arm thrust, thigh-scoop throw.
Two-handed head twists torque a man aground;
The Triple rams the chest and whips both legs.

Charge forward, building power, champions say:
Attack and grip; defense is secondary.
Be master of each ordinary way,
And ready with strange tactics legendary
To dominate divinely fiendish fray.

The Tartini Tones

"Combination tones generated by violins of good quality can be easily heard, affecting the perception of the intervals. The harmonic content of the dyad is enriched by the combination tones and this is positively perceived by the listeners."

—*Giovanni Cecchi,* University of Florence
Italian Tribune, *November 17, 2022*

by Joseph S. Salemi

Yes, it's from Cremona—we're not sure
If made by Stradivarius. Who knows?
Despite the sheer magnificence, the pure
And bell-like vibrancy, the aural glows,

There is no maker's mark. The provenance
Is vague and somewhat sketchy. It's not nice,
But dealers in old violins (to enhance
The reputation and the asking price)

Would say it came from Stradivari's hand.
And even if not true, the instrument
Might well have all the excellence, the grand
Style of that master craftsman's sacrament.

I don't blaspheme. This fiddle channels grace.
Just sit in holy silence while it's played
And hear the *terzo suono* (like fine lace)
Intertwine tones, as if you knelt and prayed

And heard angelic whispers from on high
Hinting of what the sacred seraphs sing
To Majesty Immortal. And you cry
That you are not in their encircling ring.

Those are Tartini tones. The seasoned wood
Of deep Italian forests slowly growing
Untouched through centuries, that had withstood
The chill of countless winters' frigid blowing

Alone can give that *terzo suono* mix
Of doubled, blended notes, and there's no more.
The forests are cut down. You cannot fix
That loss, just as no person can restore

The quarries of *antico nero* stone,
Avranches cathedral, Bibliothèque Louvain,
Or any precious thing for which we moan
That stupid men have wrecked, for hate or gain.

Perhaps this is not by Stradivari. Well,
We hear Tartini tones no matter who
Crafted the violin. It casts a spell
Just as enchanting as those special few.

The nameless maker of this violin
In some ill-lit workshop with his plane,
His pumice, iron moulds, and varnish tin,
Wrought voiceless wood to sing against the grain.

POET'S NOTE: Tartini tones are subtle resonances or vibrations produced by antique violins from Cremona, Italy, most particularly those from the workshops of Antonio Stradivari, Giuseppe Guarneri, and other neighboring luthiers. They were first identified and described by the composer Giuseppe Tartini in 1714, who called them a *terzo suono* ("third sound") that enriched and deepened the played notes. Listeners and recent laboratory acoustical research both testify that these tones are audibly present in the old violins, and negligible or not present at all in modern instruments. Some persons have theorized that the wood used by these early violin makers was of an unusually dense quality, as a result of the "Little Ice Age" that afflicted the northern hemisphere from about 1300 to 1800.

John Adams in Heaven

John and Abigail Adams are being guided through heaven by John Milton. He takes them to a villa in the Elysian Fields, where they meet a famous Roman Marcus Cicero, who shows them a vision of their political ancestors.

by Andrew Benson Brown

Near spartan fields that nurtured simple roots,
A villa sprawled with hints of pagan faith.
Through lavish gardens hanging with ripe fruits,
They entered, crossed a room of marble wraiths
(Ancestral busts, the mugs of common farmers)
Its murals cracked and laced with creeping vines,
And saw a sitting figure chiseled firmer
Than stone, pure morals whitening his veins.
Great statesmen all belong in bliss, ergo
John Adams gazed upon his hero, Cicero.

Stiff muscles creaked and flexed off marble crust.
Two grinding elbows moved to steady knees.
Tan sandals squeaked and shook a robe of dust.
"One needs the fortitude of Socrates
To wait for you, John Adams," uttered Marcus.
John gaped to speak. A finger silenced words.
"Just follow, or you'll soon become a carcass."
A fountain filled a pipette up two-thirds.
Sweet Abby closed her husband's open mouth.
They followed Tully down a hallway leading south.

"Three eyedrops from the Well of Life. The mind
Needs vision, too," said Cicero. They both
Leaned backward. Pupils drowned in fluid, blind.
A light-filled tunnel, granting them new birth,
Washed over John and Abby as they stood.
The busts receded from the hall. "Behold
Your ancestors," said Cicero. Instead
Of marble casts, a line of figures rolled

Before their eyes, seeming of flesh and blood—
Civilization's leaders, risen from the mud.

Stout Moses stands with tablets lightning-seared;
King David plays his harp; wise Solomon,
In his temple, strokes his even-whiskered beard;
Cyrus reclines upon an Ottoman,
Holding his cylinder of human rights;
Lycurgus promulgates his warrior code
To Spartans; Solon scribbles his insights,
Arranging Athen's laws within an ode;
Romulus picks a hill (his twin won't hearken);
The Palatine established, Brutus ousts proud Tarquin.

Augustus maps the Pax Romana's reach
And five good emperors keep it in vogue;
Justinian's wise jurists grant no breach
Of justice as he lies in bed with plague;
Next Arthur, throned on high in Avalon,
Charges his knights recite the Pentecostal
Oath, each sword around his table drawn:
To never kill or quarrel in a hostile
Manner, to flee from treason, give the ladies
Succor and rivals mercy—under pain of Hades.

This oath is taken up by Charlemagne
And mouthed by Roland, that great paladin;
The Lionheart, to honor his domain,
Embraces chivalry and Saladin;
His brother, John the Dog, signs Magna Carta
In front of all the English noblemen;
Then last, in contrast to laconic Sparta,
A queen in armor puts a global spin
On verbal virtues when, the Spanish drowned,
This Gloriana gathers bays to see bards crowned.

A Glass for My Father

Marie-Maurille de Virot, Mademoiselle de Sombreuil
(February 14, 1768—May 15, 1823)

by Joseph S. Salemi

My father was the Marquis de Sombreuil:
An old man when it happened, but back then
The Revolution took no note of age,
Of sex, infirmities, or past distinction.
All they saw was that our family was
Of gentle blood, and for that fact condemned.
When they came to escort him to prison
I insisted that I too should go—
I shared my father's blood, why not his pain?
A maiden girl of twenty-four can die
As easily as men advanced in years.
They dragged us off to La Abbaye, and there
A mock tribunal of some drunken thugs
Read out the fatal judgment: father's life
Was forfeit to the guillotine. I begged
With filial tears and pleadings. They just smirked.

One of the guards sat on a pile of corpses
Freshly slain and still warm to the touch—
Great pools of blood and gore were everywhere.
He poured red wine out for that fell tribunal
Into cups and glasses smeared by fingers
Still wet from pikes and bludgeons and curved sabers.
He took a filthy, blood-polluted glass,
Filled it with wine, and held it out to me:

Drain this glass of blood-tinged wine and we'll
Allow you and your father to go home.
Drink a toast to our great Revolution!
They smiled in mockery, as if to say
A frightened and a well-bred noble girl

Could never put a gore-smeared glass like that
To her shy and hesitating lips.
But I reached out and took it, made the toast,
And drank it down in one impulsive swallow.
They laughed with frank amusement and surprise
That I had drunk a chalice of foul death,
Looked at me with a grudging new respect,
And released us from that hall of murder.
We hurried out to freedom and fresh air.

Still to this day I cannot hold a glass
Without revulsion and a sense of loathing.
Red wine? Just a hint of its bouquet
Turns my stomach like a foetid corpse.
They killed my father and his younger son
At a later date. My elder brother
Fell in the wars that came in terror's wake.
I am the last of Sombreuil's ancient line
And in my own way, I too died with them.
I leave the world this one important truth:
You crush no revolutions with a prayer,
With votive candles or a pious hope,
Or pleas for mercy, or *noblesse oblige*.
The only thing the Revolution fears
Is when you drink hot blood before their faces,
And swear the next cup will be filled with theirs.

POET'S NOTE: About two years after this incident at La Abbaye prison, the old Marquis de Sombreuil and one of his sons were arrested again and executed by the Revolutionists, and Mademoiselle de Sombreuil remained imprisoned until the fall of Robespierre. Her remaining brother died after the battle of Quiberon in 1795, when the murderous Revolutionist general Lazare Hoche massacred several hundred Royalist prisoners who had surrendered.

Original French

«Je me fais vieux, j'ai soixante ans,
J'ai travaillé toute ma vie,
Sans avoir, durant tout ce temps,
Pu satisfaire mon envie.
Je vois bien qu'il n'est ici-bas
De bonheur complet pour personne.
Mon vœu ne s'accomplira pas:
Je n'ai jamais vu Carcassonne!

«On voit la ville de là-haut,
Derrière les montagnes bleues;
Mais, pour y parvenir, il faut,
Il faut faire cinq grandes lieues;
En faire autant pour revenir!
Ah! si la vendange était bonne!
Le raisin ne veut pas jaunir:
Je ne verrai pas Carcassonne!

«On dit qu'on y voit tous les jours,
Ni plus ni moins que les dimanches,
Des gens s'en aller sur le cours,
En habits neufs, en robes blanches.
On dit qu'on y voit des châteaux
Grands comme ceux de Babylone,
Un évèque et deux généraux!
Je ne connais pas Carcassonne!

Carcassonne

by Gustave Nadaud (1820-1893)
translated by Joshua C. Frank

"At sixty years, I'm getting old,
And I've been working all my days
Not being able to behold
Fulfillment of my wishing gaze.
I see that life on earth is filled
With perfect happiness for none.
My wish, it will go unfulfilled:
I've never been to Carcassonne!

"They see the town from up on high,
Behind the range of mountains blue;
But, to arrive there by and by,
Some five great leagues I'll have to do;
And do as much just to come back!
Ah! Had the grapes in plenty grown!
They all that yellow ripeness lack:
I never will see Carcassonne!

"I hear they see each day out there,
No more or less than Sunday's sight,
The people strolling in the square
In brand-new suits and dresses white.
I hear they see the castle hulls
As big as those of Babylon,
A bishop and two generals!
I see I don't know Carcassonne!

55

«Le vicaire a cent fois raison:
C'est des imprudents que nous sommes.
Il disait dans son oraison
Que l'ambition perd les hommes.
Si je pouvais trouver pourtant
Deux jours sur la fin de l'automne…
Mon Dieu! que je mourrais content
Après avoir vu Carcassonne!

«Mon Dieu! mon Dieu! pardonnez-moi
Si ma prière vous offense;
On voit toujours plus haut que soi,
En vieillesse comme en enfance.
Ma femme, avec mon fils Aignan,
A voyagé jusqu'à Narbonne;
Mon filleul a vu Perpignan,
Et je n'ai pas vu Carcassonne!»

Ainsi chantait, près de Limoux,
Un paysan courbé par l'âge.
Je lui dis: «Ami, levez-vous;
Nous allons faire le voyage.»
Nous partîmes le lendemain;
Mais (que le bon Dieu lui pardonne!)
Il mourut à moitié chemin:
Il n'a jamais vu Carcassonne!

"The vicar's right, a hundred times:
Foolhardiness is our condition.
Ambition leads a man to crimes
That lead him someday to perdition.
If I could find for an event
Two days around when autumn's flown…
My God! How I could die content
Right after seeing Carcassonne!

"My God! My God! Forgive me, Lord,
If this my prayer incites Your rage;
Man always grasps and tries to hoard,
Both in his childhood and old age.
My wife, 'long with my son Aignan,
Has traveled right up to Narbonne;
My godson's been to Perpignan,
And I've not been to Carcassonne!"

So sang a man right near Limoux,
A country farmer bent with age.
I said to him, "Friend, why don't you
Come travel with me, my good sage?"
We left together the next day,
But (may the Lord forgive His own!)
He died, poor man, en route halfway:
He never got to Carcassonne!

TRANSLATOR'S NOTE: Carcassonne (CAR-kuh-SONE) is a town in the south of France, as are Narbonne (nar-BONE), Perpignan (PAIR-pee-NYAHN), and Limoux (lee-MOO). Aignan (ay-NYAHN) is a French man's name. All pronunciations given are English approximations of the French pronunciations for ease of reading in English. A great league is a pre-metric French unit of measure; the actual distance between Limoux and Carcassonne is about 13 miles (21 km) as the crow flies and 15 miles (25 km) by road. The other two places mentioned are even farther from Limoux.

Byron Swims the Hellespont

*On May 9, 1810, Lord Byron swam across the Hellespont
from Sestos to Abydos to duplicate the legendary
back-and-forth trips made by the mythical Leander on
visits to his lover Hero. This was a distance of about one
nautical mile, in very cold water with a dangerously
strong current. Despite warnings not to try it, both from
local residents and from the British consul, Byron
completed the hazardous swim in about an hour. Talk
about a poet with a real pair of balls!*

by Joseph S. Salemi

What else to do but try it? Just a whim
To be a new Leander, and like him
Brave the cold strait that kept two loves apart,
And show, through daring, how a young man's heart
Is equal in real life to mythic story.
Could I not garner for myself the glory
A long-dead swimmer earned by being drowned?
Lust drove his limbs, and yet Leander's crowned
With honor, just as if he fell in battle.
Shall I not also win a prize: the prattle
Of ladies back in England who will squeal
To hear of this adventure? And they'll feel
The pangs of dreamy passion for a chap
Who's handsome, lithe, and saucy. And mayhap
They'll swoon when greeted by my rakish smile.
I'll tell them how I swam the stormy mile
Twixt Europe's shore and Asia's rock-strewn strand
Not resting for a moment, till the land
Came into view, and how the breakers' roar
Told me that I was coming close to shore.

I hardly think I'd try the thing again—
It took one hour but it felt like ten.
The water was as cold as German hock

Poured over chipped ice, and the fleshly shock
Set me a-shiver. I paid that no mind,
For if I had, I should have been resigned
To death within ten minutes. I just stroked
The waves in endless motion, as I stoked
My brain with thoughts of *Forward! Move ahead!*
If you so much as hesitate, you're dead!
And like a soldier, marching to face guns,
Who knows that if he loses heart and runs
Disgrace and death are bound to be his fate,
I clenched my teeth and kept my body straight.
All I did was swim and keep my aim
In one direction, holding to the same
With dogged perseverance. That was all
I had to cling to. Otherwise I'd fall
Into a lethal stupor and sink under.
Such weakness would have been a costly blunder.

And so I did it, and it brought me fame.
The name of Byron blazes with a flame
Unheard of since the days when poets fought
In combat, or took journeys where they sought
Adventure, fortune, plunder, or romance,
And faced men with the gallant, hardy stance
Of independent, true virility—
The kind that does not bend a servile knee
To beg small favors from a fopling master,
Or falls to pieces at some trite disaster.
Masculine, muscled poets are the types
That women love, for such men have the tripes
To seize the moment, make a sudden lurch,
And not be cowed by ministers in church
Who plead for caution and "all due decorum."
I loathe those geldings. May the devil store 'em
Deep in some dungeon in the pit of hell.
We don't need poets with the flouncy smell
Of nancy-boys tricked out like eunuch slaves—
Such worms won't swim the Hellespontine waves.

Photos provided by the poet.

1914 Sierra Honeymoon

by James A. Tweedie

A picture's worth a thousand words, they say;
A rock at Glacier Point, Yosemite.
Folks aren't allowed to stand on it today
A rule that seems like common sense to me.

Yet, there they are, my father's Mom and Dad,
Three thousand feet above the valley floor;
Together, risking everything they had;
A memory of life and love and more.

A nineteen-fourteen honeymoon where they
Climbed High Sierra peaks and camped and fished—
There were no limits then, back in the day—
When they could hike to any place they wished.

I only knew them when they both were old.
The pictures show them young, in love, and free.
And though they died with stories left untold,
Through pictures they still whisper tales to me.

Rendering Ruins

by Leland James

A barn abandoned, left to drift alone,
wind torn and breached upon the reef of time;
fields, now dust, where summer wheat was sown,
the wagons heaped with grain stood long in line

to fill the grange of this once mighty ship,
now but a shadow, listing, ghostly gray.
Raw winds and pelts of rain how cruelly whip
the wounded roof and soak the rotted hay

—the roof, an April green in days before,
a farmer's name upon it stitched in white.
This ark of kittens, bawling calves, no more.
A rat gnaws on a crib, the final rite.

Yet on this easel, raised by bardic hand,
forgotten barns, *forgotten not*, still stand.

Covid on a Clear Day

by Laurie Holding

One day I window watched for things to write;
the next day I was lost, and underneath
the spell of fever, hot, with skin stretched tight,
I slept curled up with clenched and grinding teeth.
Then came the dreams of elevator shafts
that moved from side to side, not up and down,
and misplaced babies, loosed on Huck Finn rafts.
The nightmares drenched me, but, before I drowned,
when those two weeks had passed, I stood and walked
back to my window, weak, with blurry mind
to peek outside and find myself quite shocked
that all the world was managing just fine.
My neighbors' lawns and lives seemed much the same
as last I sat behind this window frame.

Time... by Victor Mordasov, oil on canvas, 25 x 22 in.
(Victormordasov.com)

Media

by Norma Pain

You told us lies, ignored our cries.
   Your platforms you abused.
You cancelled truth; you damaged youth,
   And we are not amused.

You took big bites from human rights,
   Dissenting voices choked.
With their decree Docs must agree,
   Or licenses revoked.

But you can't hide the great divide,
   The world is waking up.
They see beyond the muddied pond,
   The overworked tin cup.

With little fuss it's over, thus…
Main media is dead to us.

Ottawa Ho!

a poem for the Canadian truckers' convoy

by Jack DesBois

In the days of yore, it is written,
All the dreamers would dream of the sea.
   But the sailor's way
   Has become passé—
It's the trucker's life for me!

How I long for the open highway!
How I yearn to be boundless and free!
   Rising up with the dawn—
   Turn the radio on—
It's the trucker's life for me!

In my sleeper cab parked on the roadside,
I'd be cozy as cozy can be,
   With the freeway's soft sweep
   Lulling me into sleep—
It's the trucker's life for me!

Oh, the solitude, how it is calling!
All those hours with no company
   But the red and white lights
   Gleaming into the nights—
Oh, the trucker's life for me!

And if ever my nation is captured
By the pirates of bold tyranny,
   I'd be there with my truck,
   To help get it unstuck,
For the trucker's life's for me!

Now, considering the fact that I suffer
From a bad, diesel-fume allergy,
   It might logically seem
   I should table this dream
Of a trucker's life for me...

And I'd likely do well to remember
My slight problem with narcolepsy—
   And my failure to best
   That confounded road test—
Is the trucker's life really for me?

Well, perhaps I am better off sitting
At my hearth with a hot mug of tea,
   Sipping "health" to the men
   Doing all that they can
With their trucks to defend Liberty.

And a special salute to the truckers
Of the land of the fair maple tree:
   Your persistence and pluck
   Make me itch for a truck—
It's the trucker's life for me!

La Bandera

A Poem Commemorating January 6th and Ashli Babbitt

"[The rattlesnake] never begins an attack, nor, when once engaged, ever surrenders" —Benjamin Franklin

by Monika Cooper

It was the feast of the Epiphany.
The mall was full, the air alive with flags
And musical with counter-revolution.
We saw the snake, never the first to strike,

The fir tree, firm as praying hands' appeal
To heaven. Banners red and white and blue
With rows of stars, flexing our chieftain's name.
Wind rolled them out like notes from trumpet's throats.

And *Nor when once engaged…* Those stars and shades
She fought for once now wrapped her like a cloak,
Flung on her shoulders in a hero's taunt.
Who is she, like an army in array?

The smoke of satan took her from our sight.
The gun recoiled to the coward's shame.
Her spirit, with Old Glory, kept on coming.
March on, my soul, with might. And say her name.

Playing with Matches

"We don't seek conflict with Russia but we are ready."
—Antony Blinken, March 4, 2022

by Aiden Casey

We don't seek conflict with Russia
but we are ready, make no mistake.
The finger that pushes the button
will not tremble, the hand will not shake.

When pillars of fire crown the silos
and tridents breach the blue depths,
we are ready with radio silence
and blackouts and camouflage nets.

At undisclosed sites, we are ready
with body bags, hardtack and guns.
We are ready for the flash and the fireball
that will glow like a thousand suns.

We are ready with iodine tablets
and letters of last resort,
with sudoku, toilet roll, sanctions
and the Int. Criminal Court.

Let none doubt America stands ready
and resolute, as in God we trust,
ready to be charred and irradiated
to a pittance of cinders and dust.

The statue of Queen Elizabeth II by Ethan Doyle White, sculpture, 2020, Elizabeth Gardens, Gravesend, Kent. Distributed under a CC BY-SA 4.0 license (Creativecommons.org/licenses/by/4.0/).

For My Queen

Queen Elizabeth Alexandra Mary Windsor
April 21, 1926 – September 8, 2022

by Susan Jarvis Bryant

My symbol of nobility, stability and grace,
Who reigned yet never ruled—she was my constant caring face
On TV screen, on stamps, in scenes of history's changing view.
She slipped away this solemn day—her time to bid adieu.

The only monarch I have loved, the only queen I've known
(This stalwart soul my heart embraced as family of my own)
Has left the throne for greater realms beyond the fuss and fray.
She's left me with a wealth of wondrous memories at play.

So on this day, I'd like to say—dear Lilibet, goodbye.
My one and only gracious Queen, please hear my grateful cry—
You shone with poise and dignity and honour and respect
In times when truth had lost its way and hope was all but wrecked…

By those who never saw the light in eyes that blazed as bright
As anthems sung in notes that rose like Windsor swans in flight.

Yet Another Exhibition Opening

*"Art is the pleasure of a spirit that enters nature
and discovers that it too has a soul."*
—Auguste Rodin

by Shaun C. Duncan

Although this bourgeois slum is flush with cash,
No decent man could ever make the rent;
So Thursday nights the galleries present
The latest styles in bland subversive trash.

Here shameless exhibitionists parade
Their philosophical banalities
To twits with ersatz personalities,
In vain and desperate hopes of getting laid.

They foul the walls with artless effluence,
A crass assault on beauty, wit and taste
Of worth to none but those with wealth to waste
On dumb, grotesque displays of affluence.

And over this pathetic scene presides
A priestly caste of po-faced propagandists,
Drug-money launderers, and smug misandrists,
Applauding as our culture suicides.

Whilst quaffing down my third or fourth free drink
I wonder what Auguste Rodin would think.

After Observing the Working Methods of a Very Important Artist

by Shaun C. Duncan

The aging fool stands deep in dirty water,
Cradling the carcass of a native fowl
To his bare chest like a tired, suckling daughter.
He wears cheap sanctimony like a cowl.
With eyes closed tight in solemn meditation,
He draws a breath in glib anticipation
Then, with a sudden, violent exhalation,
He smears the bird in muddy desecration
Across the paper spread along the bank.
This feckless skid-mark later comes to float
Upon a wall in some vast gallery,
Now worth ten times the monthly salary
Of the attendant in her borrowed coat
Who wonders if it's all a cruel prank.

No Extra Lives

by Joshua C. Frank

While all his friends were learning skills
To gain them wives or pay their bills,
John fought with monsters on a screen,
Got knighted by a game world's queen,
Amassing troves of digi-treasure
That bought eight bits of gaming pleasure.

But as the habit lasted longer,
John's dungeon shackles grew much stronger.
His friends moved on and all gained wives
While he sat gaining extra lives—
One-upped by men just half his age
Who'd put in time and earned life's wage.

One day, much older, John awoke
And felt his electronic yoke:
No friends, no wife, and children none,
His life still stalled at World 1-1.
No princess wishes to be saved
By a gaming hero thus enslaved.

John's game-themed room now seemed a waste,
An emblem of his time misplaced.
No dragon's hoard of jewels and gold
Could buy back time and youth he'd sold
For shiny bits of program code—
He wept beside perdition's road.

But, leaving home and breaking free,
He had no guide for strategy.
The social world seemed too complex
To a man who lived in pixel specks,
And so he ran back home to game,
Never quitting, to his shame.

The moral of this tale in rhyme?
Work while you're young, don't waste your time.
Don't put your life goals off till later;
Shoot down your schedule's space-invaders,
Or, like our captured gamer guy,
You'll find your life has passed you by.

EIGHT BITS: Early video games were run on processors that could only run
    eight bits (binary digits) per data block; this constraint gave rise to their
    distinctive graphics and sound effects.
EXTRA LIVES: additional chances to play, gained by obtaining certain items or
    otherwise playing well; also known as "1-ups," hence the next line.
WORLD 1-1: the first obstacle course in the first themed section of a finite
    video game using a particular coordinate system.
STRATEGY GUIDE: a step-by-step manual detailing solutions to a particular
    video game.

The Tech Addict's Lament

by Joshua C. Frank

As I take one more hit of electronic cocaine,
I snort a fresh shot of noise into my brain
And feel the cacophony's endless refrain
Charging at me like a runaway train.

I collapse on the floor, and I think, "What a drain!
I'd love to walk out, and I'd love to abstain,
But the slowness of real-space seems flat and mundane."
So, I'm tied to the tech with a thick iron chain.

An American Tragedy

by Phil S. Rogers

In his mind the purple walrus
    mutated to a bat,
its unstable form evolving
    till it became a cat.

"Old cat," said he, "you frown at me,
    it seems you are annoyed."

"I am your mind," the cat replied,
    "it's I, you have destroyed."

"This is not right, you cannot speak,"
    the man revealed a scowl.

"Like it or not, I am your mind,"
    the cat began to growl.
"Magnificent as I once was,
    my task is now complete.
I suffered much from your abuse
    now fate you cannot cheat."

"I fail to understand," said he,
    "the riddles which you speak.
So many worlds are known to me,
    it's others who are weak.
The drugs have opened every door
    that there could ever be."

"Behind those doors," the cat rejoined,
    "there's no reality."

"Where are you cat? My vision fails,
    my sight goes dark as coal."

"Your end is near," replied the cat
  "It's time to pay the toll.
You have destroyed your greatest gift,
  your musings now are past."

The man's mouth opened nigh an inch,
  before he breathed his last.

Your Agony Is Mine

What Jesus Might Say to a Teenager
Who Maliciously Cuts Herself

by Jeff Kemper

I bore your healing lashes on my back
To rescue you from your condemning hands.
Dear child, do you believe you can attack
Your agony by etching your own bands?
Your agony is mine and not your own.
Do not give in to alien demands;
Do not deface my image or my throne
And force you to a heartless *cul de sac*.

So I'll cut to the quick: I, Jesus, wept
When they told me that Lazarus had died,
And why did I say he had only slept
Yet prior to the miracle, I cried?
And no one understood. I cried for them;
I cry for you. I'm sitting by your side
To dull the edge of desolate mayhem,
And further chiseled wounds to intercept.

They knew not who I was. I ask: Do you?
I slashed the grief wherein they were detained
To show them I embody what is true:
Their agony was mine! They ascertained
When I was through, that I had borne their grief
They knew not how. The torture-stake remained,
To cut my flesh, not yours. For your relief
I died: my blood, not yours, poured out for you.

Forego the *cul de sac* and face the pain
And leave my image lovely and uncut.
Have done with vain illusions inhumane;
I own your pain, your horror I'll rebut.

Hand me your weapons; break your status quo;
And now, dear child, etch not one novel rut.
I rescued you before your birth, you know,
I bore your gashes, terror, and disdain.

Alone Together

by Joshua C. Frank

Narcissus, in the days of old,
Fell in love with his reflection.
He knew none greater to behold
And starved while staring at "perfection."
Now we're enamored with our phones
Reflecting worlds of our own minds.
We sit and stare, as still as stones,
Bound by the modern tie that blinds.

At beaches, churches, concert halls,
Campgrounds, parks, and county fair,
We shut ourselves in online walls
As at our phones we stop and stare,
Side by side with closest friends.
We shun and snub each other thus,
And our relationship descends
To that of strangers on a bus.

Groomers

by Susan Jarvis Bryant

The words the school kids speak are not their own—
Fiends mold the untrained brain till every thought
Is hostage to their noxious sexual drone.
Their toxic tongues are rife with hype that's wrought
To prey on pliant minds and sully souls—
To torture and contort truth to the core.
These grotesques push their grim and ghoulish goals
By pumping tender hearts with gender lore.
Their sick and wicked myth, it sings of joy
And wonderment that swapping sex will bring
To every transformed girl and transformed boy.
This saccharine patter hides a bitter sting…
While sugar coating chemical castration
These monsters never mention mutilation.

Pick Your Pronoun

a pantoum

by Susan Jarvis Bryant

I will not buy the lie we're being sold.
I will not play the pick-your-pronoun game.
I've seen the twisted trickery unfold.
I know the con behind the kindness claim.

I will not play the pick-your-pronoun game.
No clueless child should make a reckless choice.
I know the con behind the kindness claim—
A scheme that spurs the devil to rejoice.

No clueless child should make a reckless choice.
Lies lead to drug-and-scalpel vows of joy—
A scheme that spurs the devil to rejoice
In mutilation of a girl or boy.

Lies lead to drug-and-scalpel vows of joy.
No way will I condone this bogus care.
The mutilation of a girl or boy
All starts with pick your pronoun—Satan's snare…

No way will I condone this bogus care.
I've seen the twisted trickery unfold.
It starts with pick your pronoun—Satan's snare.
I will not buy the lie we're being sold.

Genderosity

A law providing all gender-affirming health care services at California taxpayer expense was signed by the governor on September 29, 2022, and will go into effect on January 1, 2023. It is intended especially to serve underage non-residents of the state.

by Margaret Coats

Free drugs of several kinds block puberty;
The Golden State voids liability
For anyone in perpetuity.

Free hormones are prescribed by telephone
And mailed to children young or grown or lone;
By law, all information's kept unknown.

Free travel, lodging, surgery supplied
For trafficked kids and pimps unsatisfied
With situations anywhere worldwide.

Practitioners may not cooperate
With law enforcement in or out of state;
The gold in California offers great

Prospective gain for predators and panders,
A paradise for global debauchees,
And shelter for too many crimes to rhyme.

A Villanelle for Robert Hoogland

Hoogland was imprisoned for calling his daughter female

by Joshua C. Frank

Their mouths are gagged, their hands are bound;
Their children taken by the state,
These parents have no legal ground.

While children run and play around
The lip of Hell's wide, yawning gate,
Their mouths are gagged, their hands are bound.

If they should ever make a sound,
They'll age in jail for crimes of hate;
These parents have no legal ground.

Their efforts will be quickly drowned
As red tape seals their children's fate.
Their mouths are gagged, their hands are bound.

Their children seized, locked in the pound,
Can't help them now, for it's too late,
These parents have no legal ground.

Must we raise our kids unsound
And watch them eat the devil's bait?
Our mouths are gagged, our hands are bound;
We parents have no legal ground.

I'm Not Too Keen on China Nowadays

by Cheryl Corey

I'm not too keen on China nowadays:
The moves they've made against Taiwan of late;
The way they treat their citizens, negate
Their freedoms, torture, torment, subjugate;

And heaven help the soul who kneels and prays!
The tactics used are such that all are cowed,
As fear of retribution casts its cloud,
Since Xi Jinping's the only god allowed.

I'm more a fan of China's olden days
Of tea and silks, of Chinese brush and ink,
And how the old philosophers made you think;
But now the CCP is on the brink

Of making war—their lust for power obscene.
Suffice to say that no, I'm not too keen.

Amends to the Innocent

by Brian Yapko

Dear Falun Gong, I owe you my amends.
I heard but would not listen to the sighs
Of battered souls I should have known as friends.
An Evil which I failed to recognize
I fed with foolishness. My spirit bends
To you, to never more ignore your cries.

I squandered gold. My clothes, my lamps, each tool,
And picture frame and every useful thing
I bought from tyrants. Stingy like a fool
I only thought of dollars. Everything
I purchased gave them leave to be more cruel;
For "Made in China" hides a vicious sting.

I warped my conscience. I did not pay heed
Or try to help although I heard you moan
In grief and anguish from each wretched deed
Of torture by cruel sadists. Vein and bone
Were bled and broken, genocide decreed
By soulless, faithless thugs with hearts of stone.

I traveled to the Middle Kingdom twice
For entertainment, not for education.
I sipped their tea. I ate their duck and rice
And all the while ignored their desecration
Of human souls. I paid a Judas price
And helped support a persecuting nation.

I closed my heart to you. I gave no care
For Falun Gong across a distant ocean
Defaced, defamed within a dragon's lair.
Of persecuted souls I had no notion.
My callow selfishness is now laid bare
As I bear witness to your brave devotion.

The future summons me. I failed before
To stand for right, a spoiled moral sieve.
But there are many battles yet in store
And many friends who yet may get to live.
My pen and heart are primed to fight this war.
They're yours if you'll accept them. And forgive.

Brightness of Night by Xiaoping Chen, 2011, oil on canvas, 30 x 40 in.
Description: On this dark night, a Falun Gong mother and her child
post flyers exposing the communist regime's persecution.
(Shenyunshop.com)

A Villanelle for Falun Gong

by Bethany Mootsey

The world dismisses simple right and wrong.
Like newsprint, black and white are obsolete.
Still, evil surges, sinister and strong.

"The truth is what you feel," croons every song.
Consumers catch its pitch and press "repeat."
The world dismisses simple right and wrong.

Just take a look at China's Falun Gong.
Its tenets hold no danger to defeat.
Still, evil surges, sinister and strong.

They place practitioners in cells, prolong
Their pain, and while their parts are minced like meat,
The world dismisses simple right and wrong.

A practice that once drew an eager throng
Has dwindled due to forcible retreat.
Still, evil surges, sinister and strong.

When faced with false notes, will you sing along,
Or will you scream and stand up in your seat?
The world dismisses simple right and wrong.
Still, evil surges, sinister and strong.

Honor's Song

by Susan Jarvis Bryant

I smell the Dragon smolder on the breeze.
I hear its talons scraping at the door.
I feel a gnawing shiver of unease
Torment my bones with all that I abhor.

I know the Dragon steals the very breath
Of those who will not melt within its roar.
I know it feasts on fruitful spoils of death—
Brave blazing hearts snatched by its razor claw.

The peaceful voice of reason told me so.
The stoic words of truth shone crystal light.
I know the torture heroes undergo—
I'm sickened by their devastating plight.

I feel the Dragon skulking just beneath
The fabric of our torn and ragged world.
I see its scaly form and jagged teeth—
I know its wings are wicked and unfurled.

Let's draw upon the strength of Falun Gong
To beat the beast that silenced honor's song.

Shanghai's Robo Dogs

by Maura H. Harrison

With quick unnatural steps, and side to side
Focusing glances, robo dogs preside
And prowl the streets. They wear their growls in little
Speakers around their necks, their barking spittle
A blare of words: Go home, home now, now go.
They click, record, and scurry to and fro
On double-jointed limbs, metallic bones.
They're quickly joined by dark and hovering drones
That troll the high-rise skies and reprimand
The nighttime cries for food. The drones demand
"Control your soul's desire for freedom! Do
Not open windows! Do not sing!" Who knew
That hunger's aria was humming just
Outside so many balconies, a gust
Of air that makes the starved bird scream, or sing,
As soon as darkness hides the face and wing.

Shhh…

by Susan Jarvis Bryant

Shanghai trembles at the edge of hell
As horror wafts and weaves its way through streets.
The moon melts in the flare of terror's yell—
Hot howls of raw despair till morning greets
Locked up souls locked down for safety's sake
As Satan prowls for hearts he burns to break.

He gulps the tears the hopeless start to weep
As faith gives way to panic's rise and rush.
He feasts on fear before the last-straw leap
From ledges to a fatal concrete crush.
The dreams that danced in cherry blossom air
Are caged then dashed because the experts care.

Cruel ghouls amass to grab and bludgeon pets.
The ruthless rip stunned children from warm homes.
Those imposing rules have no regrets—
They'll tread the wicked track the devil roams,
While we sit back in muzzled, mute compliance
Embracing heartless, soulless, godless "science."

Science or "*The* Science"?

"'The Science' and science are opposites."
—Richard Lindzen

by Mike Bryant

So you believe "*The* Science"? That is odd.
Science cannot be about compliance.
Scientists are skeptics. They're not yes men.
Belief's more often used to just oppress men.
Reserve belief for the Almighty God.
Skepticism doesn't mean defiance.
Science doesn't punish a transgression.
"*The* Science" always punishes a question.
"*The* Science" is no more than a façade.
Science is a strict anti-alliance
With any entities that push oppression.
All fresh expression lessens prepossession.

Parallel Man

by Roy E. Peterson

As I was going to the fair,
I met a man with silver hair.
The more I looked how could it be?
He looked an awful lot like me,
'Cept furrowed brow and walking cane.
Perhaps my thoughts were just insane.
Perhaps it was a twist of fate.
He started to communicate.

He said something I thought perverse:
"I'm from another universe."
Then something I remember well:
"My universe is Parallel."
Since we were walking to the fair,
I did not want to stop and stare.
I thought with growing hesitation
A figment of imagination

Was walking to the fair with me—
Just move along and let him be.
I realized that we were stuck
Together by some stroke of luck.
And like a shadow on the trail
I tried to lose to no avail.
If I walked faster, so did he.
I guess he wanted company.

I told the man from Parallel,
"I hope that you are doing well."
His voice was deep; his words were pointed—
"I am the one who was anointed."
I listened to the words he said:
"I am the conscience in your head.
Although you think it quite absurd,
You need to listen to each word.

94

"I have some things to say to you.
I parallel the things you do.
You still are young and I am old.
Trust in the truth that you've been told.
Our paths will always intertwine,
Since we are one of the same vine.
The paths you choose will change me too.
Be careful of the things you do.

"Now go and have fun at the fair,"
Said the man with silver hair.
"Enjoy the rides, enjoy the sun.
Enjoy your friends and have some fun.
Remember that we had a talk
And by your side I'll always walk."

Swimming with Dreams and Memory

by Pippa Kay

My childhood dreams and memories remain
through adulthood and old age. My doll speaks.
My toy car surfs that tidal wave, again.
I'm still afraid of darkness, and the creaks
and groans of our sleeping house at night.
My mother, long-dead, beckons from a crest.
She tells me not to cry. Learn wrong from right.
I must believe my mother, who knows best.

These dreams are unsinkable. They float.
They drift away. Sometimes I catch a wish
as it slips by, flimsy like a paper boat,
big as a whale but slippery as a fish.

When I make my bed these visions dive deep,
Forgotten in daylight, remembered in sleep.

Writing a Poem

by Sally Cook

Our planet moves, and so do we,
By forces that we cannot see.
Rhyme, meter always seem to track
The rhythm of the planet. Lack
Of sense or sensibility
Inhibits our ability
To see. In every fervent verse—
Loquacious, moderate, or terse—
Rhyme glues meter where it should
Be glued. The best of poets could
Unleash spasmodic movement when
Not in their normal state, but then
As darkness turns again to day
They speak, to keep the dark away.

Shakespeare by Gary Lee Price, sculpture, 2003, bronze, 53 in. high x 74 in. wide x 42 in. deep. (Garyleeprice.com)

Serious Poetry

by James A. Tweedie

Serious poetry, somber and grim;
Dashing, descriptive, with narrative flair.
   Formal and versified;
   Rhythmic and dignified;
Romance and rhetoric; ribald and prim.
Taking you places while curled in your chair.

Serious poetry, rhyming each line.
Sonnets, rondeaus, villanelles, triolets.
   Explosive hand-grenades;
   Sharp-witted razor blades.
Dangerous, edgy, designed to malign;
Rapturous beauty, inspiring praise.

Serious poetry, heaven and hell,
Painted with strokes of a feather-nibbed pen.
   Shakespeare and Tennyson,
   Dante and Dickinson,
Laugh-out-loud funny or tearful farewell
So good you can't wait to read them again.

Ode to Poets of the Past

by Joe Kidd

I do agree with the sights
    that I have seen:
the warm and comfortable steps
    where love has been

and with the sounds of truth
    that I have heard—
the whisper and the song
    between the word.

A now familiar species
    comes to bear
a message from an age
    beyond this air

    and I, tonight
do celebrate the past,
a poet in the light
    of beauty cast

    alive and free
above the crimson pain—
a spirit that must live
    and live again.

While Pondering Alexander Pope's 'Ode to Solitude'

by Lucia Haase

Grateful am I in solitude
while reading Pope's inspiring ode,
a time for pause—an interlude
           in my abode.

I'm whisked into the distant past
that once again becomes all new;
his words, his lines like shadows cast
           as poets do.

His quill, my pen—all one the same,
his chosen words re-echoing
as there burns peace within the flame
           that I too sing.

Blessed are those who write in rhyme,
a truth all poets knew or know—
those presently or in a time
           so long ago.

So here I write to have my say
befriended by a poet's glow
upon my porch this quiet day,
           my soul to know.

Original Spanish

Mañana los poetas

Mañana los poetas cantarán en divino
verso que no logramos entonar los de hoy;
nuevas constelaciones darán otro destino
a sus almas inquietas con un nuevo temblor.

Mañana los poetas seguirán su camino
absortos en ignota y extraña floración,
y al oir nuestro canto, con desdén repentino
echarán a los vientos nuestra vieja illusión.

Y todo será inútil, y todo será en vano;
será el afán de siempre y el idéntico arcano
y la misma tiniebla dentro del corazón.

Y ante la eterna sombra que surge y se retira,
recogerán del polvo la abandonada lira
y cantarán con ella nuestra misma canción.

Tomorrow's Poets

by Enrique González Martínez (1871-1952)
translated by Cheryl Corey

Tomorrow's poets will sing beyond all praise
In verse that's out of tune with present day;
New stars will bring new destinies that raise
A shiver of delight in restless souls.

Tomorrow's poets will tread a path unworn,
Absorbed in ignorance and curious tongues;
And when they hear our song, they'll quickly scorn
And toss our old illusion to the winds.

And all shall be for naught, and all in vain;
But some things never change: the youthful lust,
The mysteries of life, the heartfelt pain.

Before the shades of death that wax and wane,
They'll shake the once-abandoned lyre of dust,
And sing with her our selfsame sad refrain.

Erasing Me

by Sally Cook

As I could not do things that had to be
The practical began dismantling me.
They started with my edges; I could see
Each greyed eraser scrubbing silently.

They kindly asked if I would choose from rare
Possessions, one from each pile jumbled there.
They boxed my fur-lined slippers up with care—
Red pumps, that tapping taradiddled pair.

Some searched to find more stuff; then one fine day
My mohair shaved soft silk just blew away
In plastic bags. There were no words to say.
I took the rump-sprung robe that thought to stay.

My mind lay limp and scoured; I was a mess
Until they scrubbed me clean and clipped each tress.
I did not care for work or diet, dress—
My mouth was hollow, mute. But I digress.

As outline faded into memory,
Those myriad things that wove a life for me,
Like moonlit shadows from a branched-out tree,
Could not be grasped by those erasing me.

Two Poems

by Stephen M. Dickey

I.

Dreams are the backscatter of everything
You jettisoned, forgot, or left behind.
Sleep leaves you in their wake, wearing their ring,
Backpedaling forward, wide-eyed and blind.

II.

The hive-mind web is vying for control:
The pixelariat can bend your will
Better than proletarians, until
Nothing is real except your inner troll.

The Linguist

for M.J. Connolly

by Maxim D. Shrayer

The linguist sees the world
and takes it by the horns,
the linguist loves the word
before the word is born.

The linguist deconstructs
the mystery of sound,
he trusts and yet mistrusts;
he is forever bound.

When worlds fall apart,
when people fail to speak,
the linguist feels a spark.

He knows his sacred place:
by practicing his art
the linguist keeps the peace.

Gloucester in July

by Patricia Rogers Cozier

A thousand silent saints and angels
Hewn from vertex, plane, and angle
Raised by blow of mason's hammer
Raised from stone to watch the faithful

Underneath the sinners stammer
Pray and weep, confess and clamber
The thousand faces, gray, unblinking
Witness judgement's heavy hammer

Saints and angels in the rafters
Shadows of the Everafter
Avatars of holy power
Heralds to the day of Rapture

Climbing skyward up the steeple
Looking earthward over evil
Standing vigil from the towers
Sleepless guards of the Cathedral

Lullaby of New Mexico

by Brian Yapko

Duerme mijo—sleep my weary child
As we drive south upon the interstate.
My side-eye checks on you, my tired you.
My calloused hand caresses your wheat hair.
The radio sings dreams, strumming guitars,
The soulful voices of the mariachis
Who sing about the feathers of the dove
And fragile hope. I hear you softly snore.
We pass Socorro, hours more of nowhere.
Ay, when we reach Las Cruces what will be?
Will they decide that I'm not a good father
Because of who I was and where I've been?

I see the whirling winds and desert dust
Kicked up from White Sands and from Trinity.
We're passed by speeding cars with license plates
From richer states, from California, Texas.
But we are just from here my little one.
We drive through shadowed valleys but my heart
Says do not fear. My son, the sound of your
Soft breath is magic. I should stop the car,
And hug you. Maybe bless you with a kiss
Upon your head, but we have miles to go
To race the sun. They're waiting for us, those
Who'll judge if you and I may stay together.

The mountains cast their shadows—mighty, stark.
To see them makes me tremble for they know
To me you're sacred. No, I must not cry.
The sun shifts gold to orange in a sky
That's streaked with pink and turquoise. Even if
We must keep driving I can whisper still
I love you while you sleep. And I can say
I love you to the sky whose colors glow
With brilliant hues that look just like your soul,

Like miracles which feed my weary faith
Which will not falter; and which make me glad
To live still in this ancient, holy place.

What I Learned from Tolkien

by Brian Yapko

The darkness comes and all seems bleak and wrong,
My calm is rent, right burdens can't be borne
And Evil holds an iron grip so strong
It seems it must prevail. With all hope torn,
The path ahead seems lost in storm and murk.
But then I think of Tolkien and his work.

Specifically, his hobbits come to mind.
I treasure Frodo, who destroys the Ring.
But when defeatist thoughts occur I find
It's Sam whose decency and courage bring
Me solace. More than solace! Inspiration
And healing from these times of degradation.

It's Sam who is consistent, calm and ready
To offer words of comfort. Even through
Exhaustion and despair his sword is steady
And valor in his heart stays strong and true.
Sam speaks of stories—heroes, battles braved,
Of dragons fought, dark quests, a Shire saved.

These tales are sometimes full of so much dread
That we may never want to face the end.
What use are they when our own road ahead
Is no less harsh, when death rounds every bend?
Just this: these timeless stories help us grow
And charge our weary hearts in times of woe!

Strength grows when we tell of courageous men—
The best of who we are and yet could be.
Such stories keep us going even when
The world feels lost and hope is hard to see.
The heroes Tolkien writes are plain and bold
And won't give up or in. These heroes hold

To something—something meaningful and true,
Though overwhelmed by loss of strength and grief.
What Tolkien shares through Sam brings hope anew
And we need never question this belief:
When all seems lost, there's yet some Good in store
For this sad world. And it's worth fighting for.

Apollo in Retirement

by Margaret Coats

Quite early he approached a humble hut,
With saxifrage and canneberge sun-brewed
To melt the stone that galled the shepherd's gut,
And brighten him with warmth of health renewed.
The healer was a handsome older man,
Not much accustomed to go far beyond
Spheres where his brilliance had a dazzling span.

The Marvejols midsummer market dawned
As he unwrapped fresh simples, fragrant wood,
And seedling laurel slips. A lovesick blonde
Asked whether lovage and heartsease were good;
"Why not a touch of eyebright?" he advised,
"The sun beams long today to show how fair
This earth is, and how greatly to be prized."

"Pleasures of which you may be unaware
Derive from mental as from senses' fire,"
He tells a troubadour of ailing flair,
"But sacred sharpness fortifies a lyre.
Try hyssop, cresses, or Parnassus grass;
Stop singing of yourself—my mints perfume
Your minstrelsy, and cure digestive gas."

The village mayor's wife complains of rheum.
"Let rhubarb make your temper sweet and bold!
Your splendor and your husband's should illume
This region where you rule in rank. Uphold
Its glory, as the ancient sun still shines
Undimmed, with radiance rationally revered."
At twilight he strode home through thickset pines.

Around his lodge a pearly glow appeared,
Brighter than solstice bonfires on the hills.
His sister seldom smiled when others neared;

Tonight her artemisial aura spills
Over his hidden croft of favored plants
For physic, strowing, posies, cookery,
And healthful balance in luxuriance.

Directing random passions' harmony
Remains his aim as woodsman of Entraygues:
The surge toward strife he stills with betony;
Valerian can assuage spasmodic plague,
And music civilizes men at odds.
Hunters and farmers, jubilantly strong
Though merely human, correspond to gods.

He ventures out for midnight rites of song,
Converses with a sanctifying priest,
And gathers wisdom through hours dim and long
About the greatest who became the least.
The lordly bearer of the silver bow
Had blazed with intellect and reason but
He meets a multiverse of more to know.

MARVEJOLS AND ENTRAYGUES: sparsely populated places in the French
Massif Central.

Inviting Some Friends to a Birthday Dinner

after Ben Jonson's "Inviting a Friend to Supper"

by Jeremiah Johnson

Tonight, dear friends, you're welcome to observe
Another birthday dinner—and deserve
To know it's mainly an excuse for us
To invite friends, no gifts required, no fuss
Expected, though I will confess, I still
Take joy in marking a new year and will
Provide red wine to warm this winter's day,
With oatmeal porter further to allay,
And though I'm not a cook, I'll play the sous
Chef to my wife. We two will bake for you
A rich lasagna, with which you may pair
A side dish of warm bread or other fare,
As suits your taste. Then, gathered 'round the board,
We'll have a blessing, thanks unto the Lord,
Offered not by, but for, the birthday boy—
As that's tradition on my day of joy.
Depending on the evening's structure we
May have a fire 'round which we can see
(thanks to my brothers' woodcraft, not to mine)
A ring of faces happily recline.
And there will be a reading of some sort,
Perhaps a poem of mine, or Pound's retort,
"The Goodly Fere," Tennyson's "Ulysses,"
A psalm of David's—verses meant to please
By way of thoughtful converse—adding to
These Grahame's Wind in the Willows, with a view
To deepening cam'raderie this night.
Dessert will be a carrot cake, the sight
Of which, made out with candles, will invite
Praise of my lovely wife—necessitate
The singing of the normal birthday ditty.
Then, finally, if time allows, there'll be

Another family tradition, where
We'll make the round and each of you will share
Some way in which the one who's honored here
Has meant something to you in the past year—
No pressure though, good-natured jests allowed
(Myself already blushing, meekly bowed).
And then we'll bring the evening to a close,
The gathering of coats; each muffled nose;
Embraces at the door and wishes for
Safe travel as we see you out the door.

A Cup of Tea by Susan Paterson, 2022, oil on board, 30 x 18 in.
(Susanpaterson.ca)

Meditation

*"Say to yourself at break of day: today I shall meet people who are meddling,
ungrateful, proud, treacherous, envious, malicious. All this is because they do not
know good and evil. But I know what the good is, and what evil is; and I know the
offender, for he is my brother—not by flesh or blood, but by having the same mind,
the same divine spark.*
—Marcus Aurelius, Meditations

by Rachel A. Lott

Say to yourself at break of day:
there is a brotherhood of men.
And is it other than you say?
For they are equal, mean and spleenful,
alike not knowing good or evil.
Each to each has othered them.

But I who know the simple good
and gaze on it, as on the sun,
know this: I cannot turn (nor should)
my face from them, for we are one.
They are my Father's flesh and blood;
they wear my face another way;
they do as I too would have done,
with you, and all, had we been they.

This is the otherhood of all.
Say this, then, at the break of day.

The Drive to Reconcile

by C.B. Anderson

We never wish to eat a bug
Or force an unexpected hug,
But intimacy doesn't come without
A cost, and those who disagree, no doubt,
Are lost. But nonetheless we cannot see
Why we can't love the ones who disagree
    With everything that we believe,
    Without which we must take our leave.

We'll eat whatever dares approach—
    A fly, a beetle, or a roach—
And thank the sovereign powers up above
For letting us express our deepest love:
To watch, to eat, or otherwise engage.
Presumably we've finally come of age,
    So why do we remain afraid
    Of lessons learned in second grade?

Continuation

by C.B. Anderson

You and I are of two discrepant minds:
We disagree on all that matters—plus,
Our separate brains are not quite sure what kinds
Of things they favor, making four of us.

The four of us engage in conversations
That sound like bickering in closed committee
Meetings where doubtful fates of sundered nations
Are hammered into shape. It isn't pretty.

Despite the caterwauling that prevents us
From finding out whose foot best fits which shoe,
Much later in the night we reach consensus
And so adjourn for further peer review.

Worth Disguised

by Christiana Thomas,
High School Poet

The hammer lifts, the anvil rings,
The room with screaming noises brings
  A torture, here inflicted.

The bellows pump, the fire smokes,
A prodding chisel pries and pokes.
  This trial seems unscripted.

The flames blaze hot, the subject melts,
No pain like this has e'er been felt
  In testing, deep afflicted.

The searing kiln, the scorching stone,
Has broken to the inmost bone.
  A downfall here depicted.

In silence now, the flames dead cold
  Once melted stone
    Now precious gold.

Freedom in Forgiveness

a villanelle for Timothy

by Daniel Tuton

When chains of cold resentment in the end
Entangle souls and circle 'round to bind,
There's freedom in forgiveness, my dear friend.

When grievance woos the wounded to offend
And "justice" justified is anger blind,
We're chained in cold resentment in the end.

To slay the loathsome slayer with a pen
You thought would bring you final peace of mind,
But freedom is forgiveness, my dear friend.

On death's ill-fated threshold as you bend
With poison rage, and curse the Judge divine,
You're chained in cold resentment in the end.

But vesper light reveals a path to wend
Where self-reproach's shadow fades in time.
There's freedom in forgiveness, my dear friend.

In hallowed halls of mercy, souls will mend—
Forgiveness which the unforgiving find—
Unchained from cold resentment in the end,
There's freedom in forgiveness, my dear friend.

There Is No God?

by Michael Charles Maibach

"There is no God,"
Some men do say.
This doubt, some voice,
And claim this day.

If God is myth
Who gave us eyes?
Who gave us joy?
Who paints blue skies?

Have they no dog,
Have they no wife,
Have they no child
So full of life?

Awake each morn,
And thankful not?
Not on their knees
For all they've got?

How does the sun
Rise in the east?
Look now around—
Life is a feast!

How moves our heart?
Who made our friends?
Who made these hands
For wounds to mend?

There is no God?
Just chance and dust?
Life is in vain?
In naught we trust?

Be still your mind,
Let your heart free,
Let feelings in…
There God will be.

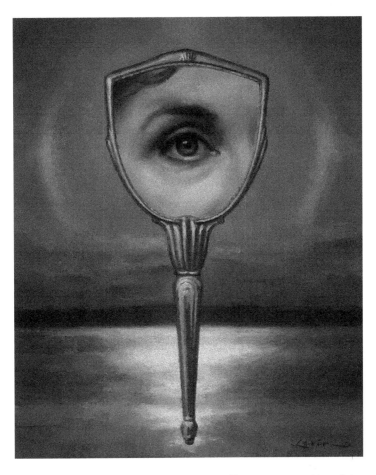

Reflection by Steven J. Levin, 2021, oil on canvas, 12 x 9 in.
(stevenjlevin.com)

"In God We Trust"

by James A. Tweedie

The motto for our nation boldly states, "In God we trust,"
Which is, of course, a matter for each person to decide.
We can't assume such faith is held by all, nor is it just
To claim it as prerequisite for patriotic pride.

But even so, the words, "In God we trust," make one thing clear:
That when we put our trust in something else, we will have erred.
For party politics will always let us down, I fear,
Regardless of which side we're on or promises we've heard.

For truth be told it will be neither liberty nor law,
The Constitution, Bill of Rights, nor some new civil war—
Where goodness triumphs at the last by means of tooth and claw—
That lead us to the Promised Land like some new Christmas star.

Though Providence has proven true both time and time again
(Despite our human foolishness) we mustn't think that we
Who dare presume we're on God's side are somehow free from sin;
For even when we do what's right, it's God who makes us free.

For by the hand of God are life and liberty endowed
And Presidents and Kings who dare pretend they have the powers
To give or take such things away have blasphemed God and bowed
Before a lie that falsely claims to own that which is ours.

I do believe that God's at work directing history,
By setting limits to the time-bound power that evil wields.
The phrase, "In God we trust" serves as a hint to help us see
That in the end it will be God to whom that evil yields.

Some trust in horses, others trust in chariots and might,
While others trust themselves, as like to Adam at the Fall.
But as for us: "In God we trust!" For such is meet and right.
For were it not for God we'd have no liberty at all.

So let us stand against all those whose power feigns full sway,
For those who claim to give us "rights" can take those rights away.

The Problem of Good

a Petrarchan sonnet

by Jeffrey Essmann

If there's (the armchair philosopher maintains)
A God (most likely writing in his blog),
Then why's the world in such a dismal fog
Of evil will and endless human pain?
Each day the whole thing just gets more insane
And sad. No god made such a senseless slog.
Our fervent prayer is but a monologue
Still rattling in our prehistoric brain.
The bigger question though to pose by far
Is how without God good exists at all;
What source by which small kindnesses accrete
To train us in a loving repertoire?
Why tend to someone with no wherewithal
Or even help some poor old thing across the street?

El Pescado

by Monika Cooper

They gloat: the age of Pisces, it is over.
They chant to call Aquarius' forces in.
In the deep labyrinths we sought the sign,
The two-stroke fish, walls clammy, glittering.

The old Mass book fell open in my hands:
The prayer for government, prayer for the king,
And there, engraved, the printing of a fish,
A fossil find, pressed thinner than a bloom.

Go, little fish. They spangled the dark pond,
Bright streaming kites, their sky under the bridge,
Over the escalator water-stairs,
Into the kettle of the deeper pool.

If anyone is thirsty. Lift your head.
I think you know the water-bearer's voice.
The bread and seafood pass from hand to hand.
My Lord, my God, are you a fish? I am.

So Close By

by Warren Bonham

At one point I was told that I
Was purposely created by
Some perfect being in the sky
Who watches as I live and die.

If that was true, I wondered why
When perched atop His throne up high
He'd let creation go awry;
I asked Him but got no reply.

I started helpless, so I'll die
But in between, I thought that I
Was one who somehow could defy
My impulse to self-glorify.

If He was perfect, why was I
Impure in ways that horrify
In ways that I could not deny,
I asked again without reply.

I'm humbled now and find that I
Can hear His whispers so close by
And see Him here in my mind's eye
Not miles away and way up high.

So, when it's I that I deny
And Him upon which I rely
I know He hears each tiny sigh;
It breaks His heart each time I cry.

Yes, when it's I I nullify
And Him on high I glorify
I'm cleansed through grace and will not die,
An unearned gift I cannot buy.

Justification

by Russel Winick

He smashed the windows, grabbed the wares,
With rage against society
That made him free of any cares
Or thoughts of impropriety.

He stole until his pockets filled
The chance of apprehension slim.
But near his home was robbed and killed
By someone angry just like him.

Uncontrolled

by Russel Winick

When my behavior needs to change,
    But I can't make that be,
Such lack of self-control seems strange,
    And I'm ashamed of me.

Sometimes the angst I feel inside
    Was planted long ago,
And all success that time's supplied
    Can't counteract back flow.

Wisdom

by Russel Winick

When young I dreamed of someday being wise,
And pictured brilliant input holding sway.
But via jolts of life now realize,
There's wisdom also in what you don't say.

Tone of Voice

by Russel Winick

The words may be perfectly reasonable,
A message which needs to be said.
But if the voice tone conveys ire or disgust,
The fruit may be bitter instead.

Do Not Return

"...forgetting those things which are behind and reaching forward to those things which are ahead."
—Philippians 3:13

by Martin Rizley

Do not return where once you were contented—
It is a trap to seal you in despair;
For time moves on, and grieving hearts tormented
By pangs of loss won't find what once was there.

Do not go back where once you felt lighthearted—
It is a snare, to lock you fast in gloom;
The house lies lorn, the loved ones have departed,
And silence reigns in every empty room.

Don't seek the landscapes or the shining places
That glowed like gold mines; now they're dark with rust,
And in the crowds, you'll see no cherished faces,
For time's a grinder that turns all to dust.

It's good to watch the burning embers glow
As slowly they grow cold and turn to ash,
But if you take them in your arms, you'll know
That only pain comes from an act so rash.

Let memories live in your fondest dreams
To make you smile as on life's path you roam,
But do not swim against time's flowing streams,
Nor seek to make of shades a settled home.

Do not go back where once your heart was happy,
The hearth is bare, the palmy days have flown,
And all your loved ones—Brother, Ma, and Pappy—
Have gone ahead and left you here alone.

Do not remain alone, but go forth boldly;
New life awaits you, if you seize the day!
For winds of cherished yesterdays blow coldly
And cannot warm you, when they fade away.

Look up! Take heart! Fresh vistas full of wonder,
New friends await you on the road ahead.
Don't let grief's vultures tear your life asunder.
Come join the living; leave behind the dead.

Original Spanish

Para entonces

Quiero morir cuando decline el día
en alta mar y con la cara al cielo;
donde parezca un sueño la agonia,
y el alma, un ave que remonta el vuelo.

No escuchar en los últimos instantes,
ya con el cielo y con la mar a solas,
más voces ni plegarias sollozantes
que la majestuoso tumbo de las olas.

Morir cuando la luz triste retira
sus áureas redes de la onda verde,
y ser como ese sol que lento expira;
algo muy luminoso que se pierde.

Morir, y joven: antes que destruya
el tiempo aleve la gentil corona;
cuando la vida dice aún: "soy tuya",
aunque sepamos bien que nos traiciona.

For Then

by Manuel Gutiérrez Nájera (Mexico, 1859-1895)
translated by Cheryl Corey

O, to die upon the open sea
At sunset, facing heaven, where agony
Is but a dream; and soul, the essence of me,
Is like a bird in flight that's soaring free.

To be already one with sea and sky,
And never hear the mourner's plaintive cry
Or prayerful sob; and if they question—why?
Majestic waves will offer no reply.

To die when the sad, fading light-display
Of haloed nets withdraws from emerald spray;
To be as the sun, which slowly slips away,
Once golden-bright, but lost at end of day;

To die while I'm still young and in my prime,
When all of life's a festive pantomime,
Before destroyed by cold, capricious Time;
Though life betrays, let parting be sublime!

This Side of Eternity

by Anna J. Arredondo

I.

Imagination, you're a two-edged sword,
The universe your oyster, opened wide;
Conceiving all the boon life might afford
In dazzling display: what may be tried,
Perpetual possibilities, outpoured
Before the casual confidence of pride.

Infinity thus beckons, but we err
Who hope to taste more than our finite share.

Ideas, lacking opportunity,
Far from propelling us to reach the stars,
Become a heavy burden on the soul—
How can a mind so vast still mortal be?
A lifetime shrinks to naught, and leaves but scars
From every hopeless dream and unmet goal.

II.

The moments swiftly filter through our fingers,
A lifetime of accumulating sands;
Despite the grip of vainly grasping hands,
They flee for good—there's not one moment lingers.
Coming to terms with each new failing strategy,
We strive to keep them, piling them in towers,
Make monuments of all the days and hours,
Only to witness more unyielding tragedy:
That time's relentless, restless turning tides
Demolish these memorials we've molded,
And ragged ribbons of a life unfolded

Adorn our empty, echoing insides.
Impossible, this dream of holding on:
The present's now; we blink, and it is gone.

III.

My soul clings to the dust that constitutes
The substance of its temporal abode—
Its shelter and its mode of transportation—
As leaf and stem cling fiercely to their roots,
From which life's nutrients have ever flowed,
And whose firm grip has kept them from migration.

With greatest pains I must preserve this crust,
For something infinite dwells in the dust.

Unlike the plants of earth, and lowly brutes,
I am comprised of more than eye can see.
In realms unknown I send up tender shoots;
With thought unbound I grow tremendously;
Ideas blossom into sweetest fruits,
Through time and into bright eternity.

Tongues as of Fire

by Phillip Whidden

If men desire to find belief, to sing
It out through throats works best to make the soul
Embrace it. This will make the sought faith zing
Behind their hearts and manliness's whole.
The faith will throb straight through the tenor throats,
The baritones' and basses' tongues, and play
Up in the tear ducts through the holy notes,
The notes made sacred by the ricochet
Of music through the body and the brain.
The holiness will well up from the lungs
And wash, as in a holy rite, each stain
Of unbelief away with concord's tongues.
  The counter tenors chime in, too, above
    Conviction like a Pentecostal dove.

My Version of Hope by Esther Huser, 2022, oil on dibond, 39 x 59 in. (Estherhuser.com)

"Where Ever-present Joy Knows Naught of Time"
—Dante, Paradiso, Canto X, D.L. Sayers translation

a rondeau redouble

by Cynthia Erlandson

Where ever-present joy knows naught of time,
The music of infinity is sung
In full-toned harmony and richest rhyme,
In higher speech than any earthly tongue.

Outside the bounds of days or hours, it's sung;
No years are measured as its deep-toned chime
Resounds with overtones, and bells are rung
Where ever-present joy knows naught of time.

Below the bells, cathedral anthems climb
To vaulted ceilings, where the voices flung
By choristers accord with the sublime,
True music of infinity that's sung

Above the arch of sky. No mortal lung
Can give full voice to it. Earth's paradigm
Must serve for now, however much we long
For full-toned harmony and richest rhyme.

Celestial choirs' eternal hymns proclaim
A ceaseless circling psalm—a perfect song
Where Evensong and Matins are the same,
In higher speech than any earthly tongue.

There, night has disappeared, and now among
The music which no longer measures time—
Where past and future, words and notes, have long
Ago become eternal, perfect rhyme—
Is ever-present joy.

Hanging Harps

"As for our harps, we hanged them up upon the trees
that are therein.... How shall we sing the Lord's song
in a strange land?"
—Psalm 137: 2, 4, Coverdale

by Cynthia Erlandson

Our harps are tangled, hanging on the trees
Of Babylon. Our hopes are strangled, dangling
From sapless branches scorched in desert breeze
That scorns our hymns; its currents strum the strings
Whose groans are haunting us from where they're hanging,
Mangling the songs we thought our memories
Would sing forever—melodies that ring
Inside our minds. This wind's harsh howls wring
The heart from Zion's charming harmonies,
Distort glad dances into mournful keys
Alien to us; these morbid chords
Turn dancing into mourning. Heartache parches
The spirit, till the mind forgets the words.
How can we sing, while our captors wrench such dirges
From long-lived festive rites? Our vocal cords
Are seared by sorrow; these once-graceful harps
Can vibrate only with our miseries
While hanging in this foreign air that warps
Their wood where they are tangled in the trees.

Taking Flight by Anna Rose Bain, 2022, oil on linen, 30 x 24 in.
(Artworkbyannarose.com)

A Holy Picnic

by Sally Cook

A small child had a vision in the light
Of day, while sitting square upon the rug.
It seemed as if she rose to a great height,
And there, her senses gave a mighty tug
As if to warn her there was more to come.
And so there was. Two men, both clothed in white
Addressed her spirit, talked and laughed at some
Occurrences that waited out of sight
In future time. Her mother saw her stare,
Her silence, shook her, cried out *Where are you?*
You look as if you're floating in mid-air!
Except for what it seemed, there in the dew
And wide expanse of Heaven, fear seemed odd
When she was only picnicking with God.

A Broadside

by Peter Lillios

Drawn up before us, proud and sure,
Costumed in their haute couture,
And sporting all the best coiffures,
With colours purple and azure,

Loom the powers of disarray,
Armed with bromide and cliché,
With which to tar or to gainsay
Whomever pines for yesterday.

Though theirs is the academy,
Our economic strategy,
Political anatomy,
And all the latest gadgetry;

So too, of course, the printing press,
The movie house, the new noblesse,
The creeds and screeds we must profess—
Lest they make public your address!

Nonetheless, as arsenals go,
Our own can surely strike a blow:
We've all the minds of long ago—
Schiller, Thales, Cicero.

Wits renowned are in our ranks;
Their words our guns, their truths our tanks.
To whom, then, do our foes owe thanks?
Why, sophists and investment banks!

Two thousand years stand on our side,
Two thousand years shall be our guide,
To make us bold and crystal-eyed
In launching every fierce broadside

Against the powers of anarchy,
Whose 'progress' lies in entropy,
And whose 'right side of history'
Belongs to rot and atrophy!

And though their might may seem outsized,
They've might alone to criticise,
To alchemise and to disguise
As 'love' their wild lust to despise.

And though, likewise, we now seem meek,
We've latent force of Roman, Greek,
Of Templars with their chaste mystique,
And all the knights of days antique.

Have, therefore, no angst or fears,
For all they wield are slings and smears
Against the might of truths and spears
And wisdom of two thousand years.

The Bard of Babel

by Anthony Watts

One eye blind with science,
The other blind with pain,
I saw the Bard of Babel stand
Out on the lonesome plain.

His fingers clawed a broken harp;
A burning song was wrung
From the vestiges of language
On the tatters of his tongue:

All you busy pimps of Progress,
Your scaffolding is rust;
Your fairy-lights are shattered
And your dreams have turned to dust;

Your breath has chased the petal
From the lens of your delight
And the flower of all your knowing
Is a flower of endless night.

And all around, the desert birds
Were screaming with desire,
As they watched ambitious carrion
Its own scaffold raising higher.

One eye blind with science,
The other blind with pain,
I heard the Bard of Babel sing
Out on the darksome plain:

Though your crippled tongues squawk lightning
As you climb towards the sun,
All your stairways end in rubble
And your race has not begun

And though I'm blind and choked with dust
And deafened by your din,
My spirit soars above your heads
And dances in the wind,

For I have been where I have seen
How all your toil is vain.
So sang the Bard of Babel,
Alone on Shinar's plain.

All your stairways end in rubble;
All your scaffolding is rust;
All your fairy-lights are shattered;
All your dreams have turned to dust. . .

The music murdered on his lips,
The quicklime in his eyes,
As lightning snickered down the wall,
I saw the Bard of Babel fall
Beneath the Tower of Lies.

The Way of the World

by Jeffrey Essmann

Some horrid truth seems now made manifest:
    Some nothingness tucked in the human core
Parades itself as fullness and the best
    In us—our grace, our reason—sore distorts.
    In mirror after mirror we adore
        A god more false than any made of stone,
        Whose heaven is a place where everyone's alone.

The nothingness, however, isn't true:
    It vaguely smells of apple and of snake,
The ethers old that make us misconstrue
    Creation's mystery as a great mistake.
    But those who know its strange Creator quake
        Before a light that strikes Unreason blind
        (And, for that matter, Reason also far outshines).

"I met Death today. We are playing chess."

—Ingmar Bergman, *The Seventh Seal*

by Royal Rhodes

In the darkened, box-shaped room
the Swedish film cast loops of light.
A knight, his windswept hair pure white
played chess upon this Day of Doom,
while meeting Death– magnesium
faced. My startled students blinked
at this figure, bored and numb
by epidemics that they linked
to barking throats and missed alarms.
I watched them as they each consumed
the mad girl caught and soldiers harmed,
soon burned for sinful sex presumed
with impish devils, as the knight
climbed the kindling — in her deep
and devilish eye could God or light
be found?– but nothing, as in sleep,
an "O" of terror, as I gazed
into the students' eyes that cast
back nothing, while my own eyes glazed,
like Bergman's dreaded atom blast.

NOTE: Selected from the Classic Movie-Inspired Poem Challenge initiated by
Susan Jarvis Bryant

The Departing Year

by Satyananda Sarangi

This night shall stand and stare with wintry rage
Through half-closed windows stained in loss and gain;
To measure all astounding feats and fame
Against those bitter tears in blinding rain.

The memories shall never wane with sight,
Nor lend to coming days a newer tone;
But serve to blurry eyes of aging time
A light to tread the path of life alone.

So let us bid this passing hour farewell,
These old, departing years shall hang on walls
Like splendid portraits of some loyal friend
Whose voice within our heart ascends and falls.

II. LOVE POEMS

Autumnal Wind

by Daniel Howard

Autumnal Wind, who are in speed as swift
As was the Spring with which my life began,
If you would sigh upon this lonely man,
And whistle through his heart's wide-open rift,
Then from the thorns of life I bid you lift
This fallen leaf; to blow me, if you can,
Across the great Atlantic Ocean's span,
Beyond whose waters, let me float and drift,
Until I bid you breathe your parting sigh,
Where first I saw my darling lover's face;
Oh blow me, blow me back towards that place,
That I may fall upon it from the sky,
And settle me, by now a dying thing,
Where I would wish my soul reborn with Spring.

—To My Beloved Husband

by Isabel Scheltens

Our married love is no ethereal sound
Which dies away when wedding bells cease tolling:
No idle lust for courting or cajoling
Which dissipates, its petty joys once crowned;
Nor yet a chain to keep the body bound,
Inured in stagnant care and yearly foaling:
No joke to sneer at, causally condoling
A freedom lost, a voyage run aground.
As yet, I know not all our love will be,
For time and we shall change and change forever.
We are but young. This is our only love.
Yet this I know: in humble constancy
We learn to love, to change and change together,
Until we, changeless, live with Him above.

Lines on the Autumnal Eclipse

by K.S. Anthony

In the depth of winter skies
Where ancient bodies hover
Moon to Sun will seem to die
When Earth divides the lovers

And in the hour of its grief,
The sun will cease its burning,
And starve the bough, the branch, the leaf
And leave the cold dawn yearning.

In the depth of dying light
The moon will cry in sorrow
Thinking that the longest night
Finds no relief tomorrow

Sun will freeze the stars to dust
Above to chain the hours
Moon will seem to turn to rust
Below will die the flowers.

And beneath their broken hearts
We question and we wonder
Where love ends and where love starts
And what tears it asunder.

If there meet two hearts, two lips
Will Earth be their undoing?
Will they only be eclipsed:
A shadow's pause in wooing?

As Earth's shadow fades from night
Rekindling their desire
Sun takes Moon into its light
And Moon sets Sun on fire

In the dark of winter skies
That oft leave passion covered
Love has often seemed to die
But none divides the lovers.

Back to the Tang Dynasty by Fei Meng, colored pencils on paper, 11.7 x 16.5 in. (Feimengart.com)

Revelation

by Russel Winick

You never see suspects admitting their guilt,
    Or partisans stating they lied.
You'll never hear soccer stars fearing defeat,
    Or macho guys saying they cried.

In a world where the truth's often hidden away,
    And the facts can be hard to construe,
One thing I would never keep secret is that
    I'd be totally lost without you.

I'm Here

by Mike Bryant

Your smile, it hypnotizes.
It rises with the Inca doves and sun.
 Sleep done, your love surprises
And spices dawn with lush and precious fun.

 Your widened eyes are fashioned
In passion that I simply can't dismiss.
 Insistent, blue and flashing
A brash and playful prelude to a kiss.

 Your words and music heat me,
Complete me with the wonders of your mind.
 Bind me to you, treat me
To sweetest odes and arias entwined.

 I know our spirits mirror.
It's clearer every year and I am still
 So thrilled to have you nearer—
I'm here, I love you, and I always will.

Little to Regret

by David Watt

When Time has stilled my body
   Think of me now and then,
Asleep beneath the wattle,
   Which flowers yet again.
And as the summer follows
   With rays I cannot see,
Let the warmth embrace you—
   My passion cannot be!

And when your time approaches
   (In many years I trust)
Be reassured my darling,
   Though I have turned to dust,
That when you lie beside me
   I'll recognize you yet,
And sleep a deeper sleep—
   With little to regret.

In the Market Square

by Morrison Handley-Schachler

Early this afternoon I was in town,
Dealing with some mundane and dull affair,
And, on my busy journey up and down,
Ran into Cupid in the market square.
The god, accosting me, since I was there,
Showed me a vision where I chanced to look
Of features, vigor, form and virtue rare
And then produced a raffle-ticket-book,
Saying, "Her charms whose face just now you saw
Are prizes for the winner of the draw.
This ticket costs your heart and your estates,
The hours of life you borrowed from the Fates,
Your hopes and your capacity for thought
And is the thousandth ticket to be bought."

Unrequited

a rondeau redoublé

by Susan Jarvis Bryant

Tonight, my eyes are open and aware.
The kiss I trusted was a lustful lie.
I'm letting go of love that isn't there.
My heart holds dreams no mind can justify.

I built a cozy castle in the sky—
A home of truth and faith and all that's fair.
But now I see a light I can't deny.
Tonight, my eyes are open and aware.

Tonight, I learned his fervent air of care
Was wispy smoke, a joke, a worthless sigh.
That burden's hard to bear. We're not a pair.
The kiss I trusted was a lustful lie.

I know the sweetness of life's apple pie—
Two feasting on a marvel made to share.
But only one felt wonder at that high.
I'm letting go of love that isn't there.

I live for love and send mine in a prayer
Together with a brusque and bold goodbye
To soothe my wretched spirit's raw despair—
My heart holds dreams no mind can justify.

I curse the sting of tears I ache to cry.
I hunger for his fingers in my hair.
I thirst to give vain wishes one more try…
But no… my soul would starve if I should dare.
Tonight, my eyes are open.

French original

O bergere, ma mye,
Je ne vis que d'amours;
Vray amour est ma vie,
Qui d'aymer me convie.
Parquoy je n'ay envie
Que sans cesser l'ayme tousjours.
O bergere, ma mye,
Je ne vis que d'amours.

Amour est ma fiance,
Repos de conscience,
Ma force et passience,
Ma foy, mon espoir, mon secours,
O bergere, ma mye,
Je ne vis que d'amours.

Amour est ma victoire,
Mon honneur et ma gloire,
Qui me faict son histoire
[Suivre] par plaisir tous les jours.
O bergere, ma mye,
Je ne vis que d'amours.

Amour a telle grace
Qu'a contempler sa face
Jamais n'en serois lasse,
Mais y treuve les ans trop cours:
O bergere, ma mye,
Je ne vis que d'amours.

Bergerette

by Marguerite de Navarre (1492–1549),
translated by Margaret Coats

O shepherdess, my friend,
On love alone I live.
True love is life's true end,
My heart can comprehend,
And therefore I intend
  My love unceasingly to give.
O shepherdess, my friend,
On love alone I live.

Love lends me confidence,
Grants conscience calmer sense,
Builds patient competence,
  Forms faith and hope restorative;
O shepherdess, my friend,
On love alone I live.

Love is my victory,
Honor, gleaming glory;
Fashions me his story
  Of pleasure's daily narrative.
O shepherdess, my friend,
On love alone I live.

Love has such lovely grace
That when I see his face
I find a tranquil place
  For fervent years contemplative.
O shepherdess, my friend,
On love alone I live.

Amour tant me contente
Qu'en luy gist mon attente.
Sa main est si puissante
Qu'ailleurs je n'en vois a recours.
O bergere, ma mye,
Je ne vis que d'amours.

Amour a soy m'attire,
Me faict pleurer et rire,
Me brusle et me martire,
Las! il me faict d'estranges tours.
O bergere, ma mye,
Je ne vis que d'amours.

Amour se mect en fuitte,
Me tirant a sa suitte,
Où je faictz ma poursuicte,
Les bras tenduz a luy je cours.
O bergere, ma mye,
Je ne vis que d'amours.

Amour, pour mieulx me prendre,
En mes braz se vient rendre,
Alors fuy après me prendre
Ses saiges et plaisans destours.
O bergere, ma mye,
Je ne vis que d'amours.

Ma joye non pareille
De chanter m'appareille;
Je crie a toute aureille:
"Aymer amours ou soyez sourdz."
O bergere, ma mye,
Je ne vis que d'amours.

Love offers deep content:
With his care provident
And arm omnipotent,
I need no aid alternative.
O shepherdess, my friend,
On love alone I live.

Love draws me lovingly,
Attracts with gloom, then glee,
Charms me with misery.
  Alas! His changes I misgive.
O shepherdess, my friend,
On love alone I live.

Love spreads his wings to fly,
Calls me to gratify
Him by pursuit; I sigh,
  And hurry toward the fugitive.
O shepherdess, my friend,
On love alone I live.

Love, to secure my heart,
Falls in my arms by art,
And then away will dart
  In dalliance provocative.
O shepherdess, my friend,
On love alone I live.

My joy without a peer
Inspires such songful cheer,
I cry to every ear,
  "Love love, or lapse insensitive!"
O shepherdess, my friend,
On love alone I live.

Bergeres gracieuses,
Soyez donc amoreuses
D'Amour, et plus heureuses
Serez que roynes en leurs cours.
O bergere, ma mye,
Je ne vis que d'amours.

Shepherdess by David Teniers the Younger (1610–1690), circa 1651-1660, oil on canvas, 22.8 x 20.4 in., The Hermitage.

Shepherdesses gracious,
For Love be amorous,
Thereby more rapturous
  Than queens of high prerogative.
O shepherdess, my friend,
On love alone I live.

TRANSLATOR'S NOTE: Marguerite de Navarre is the poet's name as wife and queen to King Henri II of Navarre. She is also known as Marguerite d'Angoulême or Marguerite d'Alençon or Marguerite de Valois. King François I of France is her brother, and the poet Charles d'Orléans, her great-uncle.

"Bergerette," meaning "little shepherdess," is supplied as the poem's title, because that is a recognized term for a virelai on a pastoral theme. For another bergerette in English, see "The Shepherdess" by Alice Meynell. The virelai is a lyric form in which all or part of the first stanza is repeated. Repetitions, like variations in line length or stanza length, can happen in a bewildering variety of patterns. Here the rhyme scheme for the first stanza is ABaaabAB, and for the other stanzas cccbAB, where the /c/ rhyme sound differs in each stanza. The /b/ line is longer than the others.

Stasis

by Adrian Fillion

It's as if we never loved. How else
To think about it? Though you've left a void
In me, oddly I find myself devoid
Of any feeling. My heart neither melts
Nor hardens at the sight of you tonight.
No doubt you feel the same. Your presence here,
Even when you pass me very near,
Is like your absence: neither dark nor bright,
Not sad, not happy, neither hot nor cold—
A passing thought or daydream. We've achieved
A stasis that I wouldn't have believed.
We don't love. We don't hate. We're just annulled.
No sorrow. No joy. No agony. No bliss.
I thought that only death would be like this.

III. LIGHT VERSE & SATIRE

In A Bind by Jacob A. Pfeiffer, 2011, oil on panel, 14 x 11 in.
(Jacobapfeiffer.com)

Sonnet to a Friend

by Johanna Donovan

It's you who've been a constant in my life
from earliest thirst and to this very day.
You've helped me sail through lassitude and strife,
have always kept the ennui at bay.

You've shown me stars and galaxies above:
spelled out their numbers, called their varied names.
Each time, whatever this heart's mind would love
to know, you've had the answer, aptly framed,

your store of knowledge, my ideal, pursued.
No matter where I've been, in you, was home.
What's more, you never once asked for your due,
except that I give back the gifts you loaned.

You've in the past and will forever be
my help, my muse, my friend, my Library.

The Errant Knight

by Cara Valle

Pictures of him at play, aged five or six,
are painful. He would always be a knight
with cardboard shield and lances made of sticks,
questing to save the damsel from her plight.

I didn't set out to domesticate
the wild swashbuckling boy in front of me,
to melt his armor into spoons, to weight
his feet with ball and chain and swallow the key.

What dreams have I unwittingly absorbed,
ground up, digested into our sane life?
He brandishes a briefcase, not a sword.
No dragons now, just three kids and a wife.

He's captive in a sorceress's power.
I want to bring him back, to set him free,
as if he were a princess in a tower.
That must be just the errant knight in me.

Crimes Against My Sanity

a villanelle

by Anna J. Arredondo

At any-given-time o'clock
While tidying my house, I find—
Oh look—is that another sock?

It really isn't such a shock;
My kids for chaos were designed
At any-given-time o'clock.

I can't tell if they try to mock
Me, or if they are truly blind
(Oh look—is that another sock?)—

They've littered every floor I walk,
Each place I peek beneath, behind
(At any-given-time o'clock),

With misplaced toys, with bits of chalk,
Gum wrappers, sticky spots, a rind—
Oh look—is that another sock?

It's hard to breathe, to think, to talk,
To settle down, relax, unwind,
When any-given-time o'clock…
Oh look—is that another sock?!!

Portrait of a Girl by Gustavo Ramos, oil on panel, 12 x 15 in.
(Gustavoramos.art)

Time Machine

by Anna J. Arredondo

Time never stands still, but the shower
Sure muffles out sound rather well—
    Are those my kids screaming?
    Or am I just dreaming?
In the shower I really can't tell.

The shower makes strife disappear:
    Are those sounds of a fight?—
    No, I'm not hearing right.
And when the kids shout that they can't live without me—
It's okay to ignore them in here.

That steady pounding on the door?
It's rolling thunder, nothing more,
Or maybe surf upon the shore.

    No needs are presented,
    No requests are repeated;
    My feelings are vented,
    My thoughts are completed!

In this gently falling rain,
I am finding peace again…

No, time doesn't stop in the shower;
How I wish it would really comply!
    It's so hard to believe
    Half an hour has passed
Before I am finally dry.

    But my soul is scrubbed clean
    As the first dawn of spring,
    And I can handle anything!—<crash>
("MOOOOOMMMMMMM!!!")
—Well, at least I'll have to try…

The Education of Wisdom

by Mary Jane Myers

Athena at sixteen: a taciturn girl,
inattentive in class, instead she's obsessed
with *War and Peace*, concealed under her desk.
Hers is not Edith Hamilton's myth. The whirl
of college, her doctorate; she flails about,
non-tenure-track, staring down career doom.
A Burmese cat and a booklined bedroom
soothe her. Drinking wine alone, her escape route,
she morphs into a drunk, "recovers," but then?
AA's fatuous platitudes cannot nourish
an idea-besotted mind. So, what to do?
Scribble sonnets! urges Euterpe, her friend.
Welcome to our bardic tribe. We cherish
Tolstoy's wisdom: the rare, the beautiful, the true!

Clerihews

from the 2022 Metrical Clerihew Challenge initiated by Talbot Hook

If I had a choice of reading Ferlinghetti
or eating an unadorned bowl of spaghetti,
I'd opt for noodles sans sauce
rather than noodle-less dross.
> —Geoffrey Smagacz

Do you remember Jerry Springer?
Each show was a high-octane zinger.
When his guests weren't fighting, their mum and dad issues
caused tear-leaky eyes and much reaching for tissues.
> —Paul A. Freeman

As an orator, young Aristotle
was renowned for a voice epiglottal.
Over time, as he waxed syllogistic,
he was deemed, sad to say, egotistic.
> —Paul Buchheit

Is it possible Robert Frost
in a bright yellow wood, got lost?
It all began when he was urged
to try to find two roads diverged!
> —Lucia Haase

The ever straight-shooting Diogenes,
No stranger to creatures' biologies,
Gave Platonic depiction a lickin'
By presenting him with a plucked chicken.
> —Talbot Hook

Snow in Buffalo

by Phil S. Rogers

Six feet of snow in Buffalo
I guess it's only apropos,
but makes me crave a bungalow
somewhere deep in Mexico.

To dance a lively fandango
on a warm and sunlit patio,
good music on the radio,
not wrapped up like an Eskimo.

Even a flight to Borneo,
so not to have to shovel snow,
would fill me with a golden glow,
and surely help my lumbago.

But all these trips I must forego,
alas, they're not the status quo;
my bank account is really low,
can't even get to Tuckahoe.

Nil Carborundum Illegitimi

by Susan Jarvis Bryant

On dismal days enswathe yourself in rays,
Then flash your splash of sunrise with panache.
Such zesty citrus, saffron spun displays
Will smash malaise with sassy solar dash—
A glowing grin that lifts your lows sky high…
  Nil carborundum illegitimi.

Brush off the bleak and bask in blasts of bliss—
A sylvan serenade will sweeten sour.
Embrace the avian aria's aural blitz
Of chirp and cheer—it smooths the grimmest glower.
Those rosy notes will boost your bluest sigh…
  Nil carborundum illegitimi.

Look beyond the bloviating blights
Who badger, bray, and bully till you're worn,
To floral, choral dawns and firefly nights.
Kick every jibing jackass off your lawn.
Don't let a cretin make you fret and cry.
  Nil carborundum illegitimi…

In other words, no clown should make you frown—
So never let the bastards grind you down.

Food for Thought

A Culinary Tale

by Anna J. Arredondo

There once was a man wan and pallid, he
Suffered from a mysterious malady:
    He ate carrots and greens,
    Ripe tomatoes and beans,
But eschewed anything that's not salad-y.

Now his wife, she was plump, but quite purty,
Euphemistically "big-boned" or "sturdy";
    Which is no great surprise,
    Since her diet of pies,
Cakes, and cookies was strictly dessert-y.

Someone wisely suggested combining
Their respective odd habits of dining:
    Then his cheeks they grew pink
    And her girth it did shrink—
The result of their palates' refining.

Don't Laugh at a Christian

by Roy E. Peterson

God looked down on Noah
And said "Construct an ark
Bigger than a boat,
More like a zoo or park."
Friends said he was crazy
Until the rain came down.
That is when we learned
The first fact-checkers drowned.

Mother Nature Is Bipolar

by Roy E. Peterson

Mother Nature is bipolar.
She needs to take a pill.
One minute she's a blowhard.
The next one she is still.
I've seen her hail in April.
I've seen her snow in May.
I've seen her sun in treetops,
Before blowing them away.

When she is calm and peaceful,
The world's a sunny place.
Her night gown often sparkles
With stars of outer space.
With breezes gently blowing;
Pretty flowers in the field,
I see abundant beauty
That cities have concealed.

She likes to visit Florida,
But then she acts insane.
She has an eye for trouble.
It's called a hurricane.
She loves to keep the people
On the west coast wide awake,
When she stomps around the region,
They call it an earthquake.

If you think she isn't angry,
Then take a trip to Java,
The Indonesian Island,
Where she erupts as lava.
I've seen her lightning crashing.
I've heard her thunder roar.
I've seen her rivers flooding
Where they never did before.

What Mother Nature gives us,
She soon can take away.
Tornadoes in the Midwest
Can happen any day.
Yet with this Mother Nature
We've declared a truce:
The gifts that she keeps giving
Are free for our own use.

By George!

by Paul A. Freeman

By George, St. George! You really are a slouch.
Arise, pick up your lance, eschew the couch.
Like Patrick, Andrew, David, fill our breasts
with pride and we shall wear upon our chests
your colours—background white, a crimson cross,
since of all saints, you're England's saintly boss.
All hail that day you struck a dragon dead
and to a rescued damsel gave its head.

With meat and ale, each year, we'll hold a feast
to mark St. George's slaying of the beast,
cry, "Rorke's Drift! Nineteen sixty-six! The Rock!"
to fish and chip shops, pubs and maypoles flock.
Forget all dull engagements, join our herd
of Anglophiles on April twenty-third;
for English folk have found the saint they seek,
no matter that the fellow was a Greek.

PATRICK, ANDREW AND DAVID: Patron saints of Ireland, Scotland and Wales, respectively.
RORKE'S DRIFT: The Defense of Rorke's Drift, in 1879, was a military engagement during the Anglo-Zulu War.
1966: the only time England have won the World Cup for football (soccer).
THE ROCK: Gibraltar, a much disputed British overseas territory on Spain's south coast.

Benjamin Franklin Drawing Electricity from the Sky by Benjamin West
(1738-1820), c. 1816, oil on slate, 13 3/8 × 10 1/16 in.

Lightning Ben

an excerpt from Legends of Liberty, Volume 2

by Andrew Benson Brown

Ben Franklin's scientific senses swelled
When lightning struck his kite and killed him dead.
Onlookers swear his final breath expelled
A soul that lingered, flit about, and fled
To Hell. This fool had played with heaven's fire
And quite deserved the fate he had received.
A person who'd conduct a test so dire
With hopes to not get burned was much deceived.
Some children ran up and began to poke
The crispy corpse, when *lo!*—Immortal Ben awoke.

He sat up, shook his head, and looked about.
His hair stood wild on end, his clothes were singed,
His face was flushed, his veins were bulging out.
A woman, seeing grey irises tinged
With yellow, fainted. Probing youngsters prone
To mischief screamed. A preacher yelled, "He deals
With demons!" Like a tree that sprouts full-grown
From fertile soil, Ben sprung upon his heels
And said with eager eccentricity,
"Eureka! I've discovered electricity."

Men came with linen bags and brimming pails.
"Who set a fire?" yelled the Bucket Brigade.
Hospital staff, their pallid hats like sails,
Blew in: "Is someone wanting a band aid?"
A small police force beat anxiety
With brandished sticks: "Which culprit needs locked up?"
The Philosophical Society
Inquired: "What person's deeds could be chalked up
To vices causing reasoning to flounder?"
Each group received its answer: their dynamic founder.

Ben's shoes sent currents through the cobblestones
He'd paved. They rippled through the city grid,
Lighting the streetlamps he'd installed in zones
Of commerce—marvelous! Time to forbid
Whale hunting—burning oil was obsolete.
(This epic is environmentally
Aware). House windows, lit up from the street,
Showed mothers tucking, sentimentally,
Their children into bed, then blowing candles
Out—be careful! Curtains catch: disaster kindles.

The crowd was following as static zapped
Between them. "Au!" A German immigrant
Cried out. He shocked an Irishman, who slapped
A Scot, who jumped. A brawl was imminent.
Shops emptied. Taverns filled as the sun went
Down. Puritans from Boston echoed, "Ben's
A witch!" Quakers replied: "Be tolerant."
Benevolence, that binding good, will cleanse
Men's souls who join the City of God—someday.
Till then, the one of Brotherly Love is here to stay.

The melted kite was trailing from a string,
All frazzled, stuck to Franklin's shoe. It snapped
While closing his front door. An urchin ring
Fought for the remnants of the kite and clapped.
The mob went separate ways. There in the dark,
Ben peeked out through the window. No eavesdropping.
He lit a candle with a finger spark,
Then read a note that Deborah left: "Gone shopping."
He sat down in his research laboratory
And tapped the frontal lobe of a *memento mori*.

The Modern Cardinal's Song

after "The Major General's Song" from Gilbert &
Sullivan's The Pirates of Penzance

from a faithful Catholic scandalized at the men
purporting to lead the Church

by Adam Sedia

I am the very model of a modern Catholic cardinal,
I've passions homosexual, heretical, and criminal,
I know no old Church Doctors and I quote facts ahistorical.
From Peter to Roncalli I've disinterest categorical.
I'm well-acquainted, though, with ideologies political:
I know the Marxist doctrine, theoretical and practical;
Of critical race theory I'm teeming with a lot of news …
With a lot of fancy language that I lifted straight out from Marcuse.
I'm very good at smashing up and painting over sacred art
And putting up monstrosities upon the shrines I tore apart.
In matters homosexual, heretical, and criminal,
I am the very model of a modern Catholic cardinal.

My preaching on morality is anything but orthodox:
I give the sacraments to anyone who'll fill my tithing box.
I imitate with gusto all the crimes of Heliogabalus
And thrill with pride when all the drag queens call my gay Mass
　　"fabulous."
I liken all my critics to the carping scribes and Pharisees
And marvel that I have no new vocations in my diocese.
Then I can belt some cheesy show-tunes masked as hymns like none
　　before …
But ban those ancient chants that my gay liturgists find such a bore.
Then I can write a check to settle sex abuse and kiddie porn,
Forgetting that I hid the facts and silenced all who tried to warn.
In matters homosexual, heretical, and criminal,
I am the very model of a modern Catholic cardinal.

I preach for open borders and can fit them in the Parables.
I hang abstract felt banners, I've a taste for tribal chasubles.
When in restricting Latin Mass I'm most authoritarian,
And when I know the detailed sex life of each seminarian,
When I praise women's progress in the Swedish episcopacy,
When I know more of back-room deals than all the lobbies in D.C.,
In short, when I've a smattering of watered-down theology ...
You'll say a better cardinal has never overseen this see.
For my theologic knowledge, though I'm plucky and adventury,
Has only been around since the end of the last century.
In matters homosexual, heretical, and criminal,
I am the very model of a modern Catholic cardinal.

Original Romanesco

Papa-Leone

Prima che Ppapa Ggenga annassi sotto
A ddiventà cquattr'ossa de presciutto,
Se sentiva aripete da pertutto
Ch'era mejjo pe nnoi che un ternallotto.
Cquer che fasceva lui ggnente era bbrutto,
Cquer che ddisceva lui tutto era dotto:
E 'ggni nimmico suo era un frabbutto,
Un giacubbino, un ladro, un galeotto.
Ma appena che ccrepò, tutt'in un tratto
Addiventò cquer Papa bbenedetto
Un zomaro, un vorpone, un cazzomatto.
E accusí jj'è ssuccesso ar poveretto,
Come li sorci cuann'è mmorto er gatto
Je fanno su la panza un minuetto.
—Volume I, poem 487

Pope-Lion

by Giuseppe Gioachino Belli (1791-1863)
translated by Joseph S. Salemi

Before Pope Genga went down to the grotto
To be four slabs of cured ham on the bone,
He was thought by everyone in Rome
To be our best luck since the jackpot Lotto.

What he did seemed never to be bad;
What he said seemed always to be wise—
His every foe a creep you could despise:
A Jacobin, a thief, a worthless cad.

But just as soon as he died, in a wink
That highly praised and blessèd Pope became
A jackass, an old wolf, a babbling stink.
And so it happened to the poor guy's shame

As mice do when the cat's dead: smile, strut, blink,
And dance a little jig on his cold frame.

TRANSLATOR'S NOTE: Many of Belli's sonnets touch directly upon individual popes, either critically or comically. This one ("Papa-Leone") is about Leo XII, who was a contemporary of Belli.

"Papa-Leone" was Annibale Della Genga (1760-1829), who reigned as Pope Leo XII from 1823 to 1829. A compromise candidate who was elected late in life (he did not want the position), he was unpopular in both the city of Rome and the surrounding Papal States. He had shown good will and administrative abilities in his earlier diocesan appointments, but he was completely out of his league in the much greater and more complex task of handling the vast territories of central Italy.

Leo XII tried hard to maintain a semblance of order and a veneer of respect for the papacy, and in Rome he was strict in suppressing any open dissent or criticism. But Italy during his pontificate was seething with discontent and troubles, and all Leo could do was try to maintain the status quo and pass the difficulties on to his successor. Belli's sonnet reveals the anger that lurked below the calm surface, and that erupted on the Pope's death.

Belli's title is probably a sarcastic slap at the Pope's ineffectiveness or lack of strength as a politician. The word leo means "lion" in Latin, and the normal reference in Italian to this Pope would be "Papa Leo," but by calling him "Papa-Leone" (which uses the standard Italian for the animal) Belli emphasizes, with a certain contempt, the man's inability to show the guts and courage required to be a real ruler. Calling him "Ppapa Ggenga" in the first line probably adds to the disrespect, since referring to a Pope by his family name is always demeaning.

Nevertheless, Belli attempts to be even-handed—his octet mentions that the election of Pope Leo did at first fill Romans with hope, and many of his incidental acts seemed useful and wise. But the concluding sestet can be taken in two ways: either the Roman populace was so fickle that the slightest thing could alienate them, or the subjects in the Papal States slowly began to realize that Pope Leo's only aim was to sit things out and do nothing substantial for their benefit. Whichever the case, Pope-Lion lost his reputation quickly, like a dead cat.

Some Vocabulary Items

presciutto: standard Italian *prosciutto*, a cured pork product.
frabbutto: standard Italian *farabutto*, scoundrel, creep.
giacubbino: a radical, a liberal (English and French "Jacobin").
vorpone: standard Italian *volpone*, an old and dangerous wolf.
cazzomatto: literally a "demented prick," and in Italian the term signifies a stupid, blundering blockhead, with the associated meaning of a brutish ruffian.

Time Is of the Essence

by Norma Pain

The powers that be in their ivory tower,
Make important decisions for sure,
While the rest of us mortals surrender our power,
We conform… we adapt… we endure.

I refer to the wisest decision of all,
Introduced by our leaders so bold,
Affecting each timepiece, each clock on the wall,
To our betterment so we are told.

We move the time forward an hour in the spring,
In the autumn we move it on back.
Please don't try to question, no conjecturing,
Our leaders are never off-track.

It's all very simple, just follow the rules,
Spring forward; fall back, right on cue.
Don't say that we must all be limp-minded fools,
Even though this might be true.

Time is of the essence, of this there's no doubt,
Let the powers that be have it known,
We haven't a clue what this thing's all about,
Why can't we just leave time alone?

Dr. Quack

by Norma Pain

My name is Dr. Henry Quack and in my little room out back,
Are lots of pills and potions.
There's drugs for this and drugs for that; if you're too skinny or too fat,
And drugs to cure emotions.

I've studied books and bones and charts, learned all about the body
    parts,
And countless medications,
And if I act as drug promoter, do my job and make my quota,
I can win vacations.

Forget the veggies, nuts and seeds, drugs are what your body needs,
Have no hesitation.
Pop a pill, take two or three; good for that arthritic knee
In any combination.

Exercise… a healthy diet, it's a waste of time to try it,
It won't cure your ills.
I believe a better way, is medication every day,
Just keep on popping pills.

Some people think too many sweeties might be causing diabetes,
This is just misleading.
Science has the final say, drugs and needles every day
Is what your body's needing.

For every ache and pain and throb, your drug of choice will do the job,
Treat every pain you get.
Just mix and match and you'll be glad, one word of caution I must add,
Don't give them to your pet.

These yellow pills will cure your ills, they'll take away your aches and
    hills,
And leave you feeling mellow.

They'll calm your cough and soothe your throat, they've got a tasty
    sugar coat,
Remember that they're yellow.

These little red ones, nice and round will guarantee a sleep that's sound,
    Or if the flu should chill you.
Take one before you go to bed, remember they're the brightest red,
    Take two or more… they'll kill you!

I'm Dr. Quack, I'm here to help, forget the flax seeds and the kelp
And all those nutraceuticals.
Drugs will get you feeling healthy, cure your pains and make me
    wealthy,
Embrace pharmaceuticals.

Cat Versus Christmas Tree

by Roy E. Peterson

The house cat was excited:
At what was in his room.
It looked just like a tree,
And smelled like pine perfume.

The cat thought to himself,
This must be my reward.
Perhaps my family knew
That I was getting bored.

Another miracle
Appeared before his eyes:
They'd decorated it
Much to his great surprise.

They hung up pretty balls
That swung to and fro,
Then strings of blinking lights
That had a pretty glow.

Then they tried to warn him:
"Do not play with that,"
But they don't know the longings
Of a pussy cat.

Pretty packages
Like dancing sugars plums
Were left there in the room.
He thought: "My chance now comes!"

He batted the first ball he saw
On the lower limb.
It had a fun reflection
That looked a lot like him.

Time to climb up in
The boughs of this pine tree;
To see what made that blink,
And study it closely.

He climbed up to the top;
Then chewed upon a wire.
The cat received a shock
That stung his mouth like fire.

He scrambled in the boughs,
And jumped immediately.
Crashing down on him,
Fell too the Christmas tree.

The family came arunning
"What terrible sound was that!?"
And there beneath the tree
They found fried pussy cat.

Christmas Rules and Promises

by Roy E. Peterson

My first rule for this Christmas is
    No carrot sticks for me.
They might have been a snowman's nose,
    So I will let them be.

My second rule this Christmas is
    Your gift I will remember;
So if it turns out kind of cheesy,
    I'll match it next December.

My third rule for this Christmas is
    Don't change the songs I play.
When you are in my house you must
    Endure them for the day.

I'll gift-wrap empty boxes nice,
    Then give a warning dire.
If you won't listen, or obey,
    I'll throw one in the fire.

And if you breathe a bad word to
    My Christmas company,
I'll douse your head with eggnog,
    Throw you through the Christmas tree.

Politely say "Thank you" for every
    Photo, gift, or box,
Even if it's handkerchiefs
    Or just a pair of socks.

You'll wish to all a "Merry Christmas,"
    When meeting them this yule.
That is my final Christmas wish,
    And final Christmas rule.

The Spoonerisms Man, or
The Moonerisms Span

by Jeff Eardley

His name was Mr. Spooner and he owned a service station.
He kept our vehicles on the road, a noble occupation.
So handy with the oily rag, the torque wrench and the socket,
Who knew so well the mysteries of pulleys, gears and sprockets.

But poor old Mr. Spooner had a notable affliction,
He tangled and he mangled every aspect of his diction.
"Your star, it will not cart," he cried, "Your flattery is bat,
You need a chattery barger, I can take good care of that."

It's then the old man gave a sneeze that covered me with spume,
I thought my Covid days were done, I thought I was immune.
But surely, he'd infected me, my words had turned around,
I started speaking just like him, a most disturbing sound.

The old mechanic stared at me, a flat cap on his head,
I'd have to pay his hefty bill, my mind was full of dread.
"I do not have a plaster man, my money is all gone,
The rental on my shiny tack makes sure that I have none."

That night, I hurried home at speed, on foot, it proved a slog,
To dine and shake a tower, take a nap and deed the fog.
My driving days are over now, I travel nice and slow,
Upon a well-boiled icicle, 'tis such a blushing crow.

Quatrains

by Russel Winick

Definitions of a Woman

It defies basic science and logic,
But we've learned with the swimmer from Penn,
To the Left there are two types of women,
Biological women—and men.

One-Sided

When you hear a person express discontent
In a statement quite un-laudatory,
It's troubling, but know that's one hundred percent
Of just fifty percent of the story.

Useful Instruction Manual

The manual that came with his new hearing aids,
Said if he'd like to still hear something clearer,
One strategy that's worked quite well for decades—
If possible is get up and move nearer.

CBS Has Now Verified

CBS says it's now verified,
The laptop Hunter took in for repair.
And other breaking news that it's supplied
Is Washington has crossed the Delaware.

Qualifications

I'll believe society has
Reached the proper track,
When outcomes are derived from skill,
Not skin that's white or black.

Standards

Is it old school
To expect the propriety
Seemingly waning
In modern society?

Publication Probability

When journals that publish your meter and rhyme
    Feature nothing remotely alike,
It's probably just a short matter of time
    Until they tell you "Go take a hike."

199

A Tribune to Mrs. Malaprop

by Brian Yapko

My fellow poets, lend me your arrears!
Of arms and divan I sing. Let's have three cheers
For Mrs. Malaprop, that dole enchanting
tongue-tried Miss Communicating aunt
From Sheridan's old comedy of mangers.
She spoke with verbal and linguini dangers.
Her word-choice wasn't always quite erect
Nor sentence glamour fully circumspect.
But do not mealy view her speech askance
For, like great masters of Reconnaissance,
The words she drew came dully from the heart
Like Botticelli's greatest warts of art!
To honor her I've gartered a few samples
Of malaprops—enjoin some free examples:
Now is the winter of our disco tent
So full of sound and furry, heavy-sent.
The better part of valor is distemper
So best to never file into a temper
Or weigh what roguish fools these morsels be!
As beverage is the sole of wit, we see
A timely rising tide will lift all bloat
And all swell will end swell, as Shakespeare wrote!

If you disliked these get thee to an ornery!
You'll find no butter puns in a reformery.
Alright, my fronds! Please cease tomato flinging!
I am a man more sinned against than singing!

An Oldie's Valentine Love Poem

by Jeff Eardley

We met when she was seventeen,
The fairest maid I'd ever seen.
With eyes of blue and flaxen hair,
My mouth agape, I had to stare,
And wonder, if a girl like she,
Would ever choose a fool like me.

But now she's just reached seventy,
And I'm still where I'll always be.
I try to quell her doubts and fears,
Just like I've done for all these years.
The anxiousness she often gets,
When browsing on the Internet.

We never argue, never fight,
We must be doing something right.
From crocus poking through the snow,
To Summer's dreamy afterglow.
Aquarius and Gemini,
It seems to work, I don't know why.

We have no need of Valentines,
Expensive meals and dodgy wines.
With waiters looking down their nose,
In dinner suits and dicky-bows.
We'll cuddle by the fire instead,
A glass or two… then off to bed.

Abiding Senescence

senescence: the state of being old

by C.B. Anderson

My energy and physical abilities
Will not again be limitless as once they were.
To those more qualified to ponder facts like these,
Without a single qualm or doubt I will defer.

They tell me I should try to get more exercise,
To do my best to modify my present diet,
And never imitate those other aging guys
Whose only keen desire is for some peace and quiet.

I've gone with almost everything these dons prescribed,
Including capsules filled with powder from some fungus,
And who can say how many flagons I've imbibed
While 'scrying contours through a flimsy cotton sundress?

They tell me that I've somehow failed to comprehend
The nuances of all the wisdom they've imparted,
That had I followed through, I'd now be on the mend—
Instead, they say, I've gone right back to where I started,

Which more or less is what I wanted all along.
I've never been submissive or obedient,
And I have earned the right to do a few things wrong,
Especially if I find such deeds expedient.

They promise that in time some things will get much better
If I will just attempt to be what I am not.
I'd follow all their precepts to the very letter,
But time is something that I haven't really got.

Back in My Day

by David Whippman

I tested my courage—well, no, not really.
The heroic stuff had been done before.
My generation was all touchy-feely.
It was our parents who'd fought the war.

The post-war population bulge:
I have to admit we did pretty well.
No combat stories to divulge,
No austerity tales to tell.

Not for us the rifle drill,
The sight of bombers on the wing.
Our time was rock'n'roll and the pill,
When society began to swing.

Our forebears, they were tough all right.
But by the time *we* came along
The only battles left to fight
Were those found in a protest song.

Our lives were soft and safe and longer.
We lose out in just one way,
We cannot say to someone younger:
"Things were much harder in *my* day."

Icon of the Bridger Mountains by Robert Schlenker. (Robertschlenker.com)

Pets and People

by Julian Woodruff

Do cats and kittens ever wonder
Why their owners have no fur?
Do dogs think it was blind fate's blunder
That the likes of humans were
Afflicted with this vile condition,
Curse of their unique position
On this crazy planet earth?

Or do all furred ones, rather, think:
Those humans are so cool, so fine
And surely I am on the blink.
For furlessness, oh how I pine!
I wish those humans could not see
Poor old, pathetic, hairy me!—
Betide with woe, bereft of mirth?

No, no, we value pets because
They're sensible. They'd all go far,
Respecting all of Nature's laws,
To keep things just the way they are.
Their fur's okay by them. And should
They sometimes fix a gaze on you
That hints, I'll tell the neighborhood
What you look like, don't worry: few—
No, none—deplore your skin (or height, or girth).

On Sighting a Marsupial

"Serve with: Turnip greens" —Joy of Cooking

by C.B. Anderson

Opossums are so ugly that it isn't clear
Another of their kind would find one good to look
At. Matted fur and hairless tails do not endear
Them to Americans. According to a book

I read, their closest relatives are found down under—
Such animals as winsome kangaroos and cute
Koalas —causing a reflective man to wonder
If maybe they were shipped abroad by some astute

Australian aborigine who recognized
Our vast emergent Melting Pot for what it was,
Or whether maybe Mother Nature so despised
Her homely get she sent them packing—or because

She just adores a vacuum. In the middle of
The night I watched a possum gnaw the chicken bones
Intended for my cat. My heart holds little love
For uninvited creatures feasting in the zones

I guard. I'm all for immigrants if they are legal
And don't pretend, as these, to be what they are not:
They're good at playing dead, and may deceive an eagle
But not coyotes which, like them, are often shot

On sight.

CDC: Save the Planet from Poison CO2!!

"We used to think CO2 was a harmless trace gas…
How wrong we were!"
—Dr. Dillard "Sparky" Barker, SMFS,
The CDC's Second Most Famous Scientist

by Mike Bryant

Your noxious exhalations contain tons of CO2
So Dillard "Sparky" Barker has the newest mask for you.
It's built to capture greenhouse gas and lock it in a filter
So that your breath won't kill the earth, and kick this sphere off kilter.

Help us fight emissions, let's douse our climate pyre.
Don't walk, don't talk, don't blink, don't breathe, don't be a dumb
    denier.
We're confiscating gasoline and rationing food and power
And water too… don't swim, don't bathe, don't flush or take a shower.

Feel the fear, the end is near, we're all in this together.
Pay the cost, it's worth the pain to change inclement weather.
Let's crush the curve, mask up, it's just a short and sure-fire lockdown.
We will stamp out Carbon Crime, we'll triumph with a Knockdown!

The Simplest Way to Save the Earth

by James A. Tweedie

The simplest way for us to save the earth
Would be for women to stop giving birth.
For when there are no longer any mothers
We'll solve the problem of too many "others."

The truth in this is easy to deduce:
As long as people mate and reproduce
As fast or faster than they are deceased
Environmental impacts are increased.

For animals and plants are not polluters,
It's people who are carbon-spewed commuters.
The quickest way to prove we love our planet
Would be to cancel intercourse and ban it.

Then all whose reproductive rates are zeroes
Will be acclaimed and lifted up as heroes.
While women who have children will be blamed
While also being canceled, mocked, and shamed.

With social values all turned topsy-turvy,
And pregnancy deemed worse than having scurvy.
We'll know the world's salvation's nearly there
When we're reduced to one last mating pair.

And when that final human pair have passed,
The earth will be restored and healed at last—
An Eden, pristine, beautiful and fair—
With no one left to see it . . . or to care.

In a Soviet Gulag

by Evan Mantyk

There was a break in the relentless cold
And then the guard stepped out for quite a while.
Such changes made the prisoners grow bold:
Two yelled their thoughts, another cracked a smile.

One wanting to impress the others told
Of how he landed there, "I once opposed
The fierce Kaganovich." Then silence rolled
Over the room, though one mouth wasn't closed:

"Well I had thought Kaganovich was gold
The Party wouldn't sell, but now I'm here
For my support of him. When things unfold
You never know which side's the one to fear."

They laughed except one in the corner which
Said morbidly, "I am Kaganovich."

Redbeards

by Damian Robin

Karl Marx had a bigger beard than Engels.
Engles had a bigger beard than Lenin.
Lenin had a bigger beard than Stalin
Who had no beard, just a lip of wangles.

Stalin's 'stache was two huge laughing roaches
That he hoped showed him more a man than Mao
Whose smooth moon face, full udder of a cow,
Has been the hook for followers' approaches:

So Bosses of the Party go clean-shaven
(Though they're not clean inside nor anywhere).
They frown on full-flown forms of facial hair,
Use cut-throat blades to keep their image graven:

The CCP's so scared of losing face,
Its leaders won't leave one hair out of place.

Asinine

to atheist evolutionists

by Damian Robin

When your science cannot put to rights
The special wrongs of our divinity,
Your exasperation reaches heights
That challenge all the laws of gravity.

When you talk at us and see our hearts
Are strong on blind belief and Godliness,
Though we are more than sums of our seen parts,
You tar us with unknowing ugliness.

You want to stick us tightly to one spot
Where no amount of feathers help us fly,
Demand we acquiesce to what we're not
According to your science that we defy.

No heaps of calling us an ass or donkey
Makes you or I descendants of a monkey.

An Anti-Evolution Song

inspired by the writings of Zhang Tianliang

by Evan Mantyk

How probable is it, however you spin it,
    That man has evolved out of nothing?
Do I look like a schmuck who would think that dumb luck
    Could just randomly tweak and make something?

Here's where most will call "God!" but that's even more odd
    Though it helps you avoid ruffling feathers.
Since this theory is broke such a "God" is a joke
    Who's restricted by bumbling tethers.

There's evidence lacking to give proper backing
    To each intermediate step
In Darwin's menagerie—it's a catastrophe
    Biologists quietly schlep.

With logic that's circular they're always particular
    On advances that ancient man made;
Their timeline is crucial so anything unusual
    Must into their framework be laid.

Just as humans defy the animal cry
    For survival of only the fittest,
They race to explain with infinite pain
    "Something changed"—though they haven't a witness.

You are flawed fundamentally when you essentially
    Require all science on your terms;
While you think and you think into hubris you sink
    And to pettiness tiny as germs.

Your demands of an answer are those of a cancer
    Unreasonably growing in size;

Although you feel cool, Common Sense would yell "Fool!"
    As you rush to fill gaps up with lies.

Suppose you are walking (quite different from Hawking)
    And find there's a fine writing table.
You conclude it's oak wood, that the craftsmanship's good,
    And screws made of steel keep it stable.

It says "Made in France," which seems a strange chance
    But otherwise you're satisfied;
You know where it's from and the parts of its sum
    And in knowing you feel gratified.

But that's not the whole picture, it's merely a tincture
    Compared to the table's real tale
Of man's need to write, and perennial plight
    To organize life without fail,

To forge a great nation and civilization
    Where language is written from thought;
Of the need to believe that the words we conceive
    Should be written and won't be for naught.

Take any away and the table won't stay;
    It's created on levels more deep
Than what you can measure or hoard as your treasure—
    I shepherd while you play with sheep.

Think (Ideo)logically

by Daniel Magdalen

Say—friend or foe? What else could people be?
… Stop thinking, since it's useless, and it's hard.
We'll do your thinking *for* you—play our card!
These glasses will now show you what to see:

This world's in black and white. We've gauged its worth.
Here's all our speeches—your beliefs, our merch.
Laugh off what experts tell you. Don't research.
Come chant our slogans—*these* shall guide you forth.

Our merits? All beyond the present lie;
Our great results are always *soon* to come!
But why not now? Because some rotten scum
Would thwart our efforts and subvert us (sigh).

Our economic plan's been snatched… But get
Some napkins ready—we'll devise one more.
They've also dragged us in a media war:
We're blamed for things we haven't done! (Just yet.)

They've silenced us with slander. We're abused
Because of our great goals. It's only fair
The people's righteous wrath that they should bear—
"Fight fairly, in good hate!" Misdeeds? Excused.

Not sure what's true? In search of solid ground?
Times shape the truth like sea waves shape the sand.
Support our foes, and man shall swindle man;
But if we win, we'll turn that all around!

Alive or dead, you'll join our lofty fight
And vote, so all we say becomes the truth!
We're great, yet modest. Though it sounds uncouth,
It just so happens that we're always right.

Hell Rising

by C.B. Anderson

They've come with a purpose: to numb or perturb us
  By infecting the already-sick,
And with them they bring a more tangible thing:
  A nice carrot along with a stick.

They live in The Palace of Envy and Malice
  And demand that we pay our "fair share";
Regarding new taxes, their mantra *Relax!* is
  Just to make us forget that we care.

They sneer at our morals and tell us that plurals
  Go beyond normal binary modes;
They say that a city looks best when it's shitty
  And let excrement pave all the roads.

But that's not enough: When the going gets tough
  They declare it the businessman's fault;
While wounds freely bleed, they attend to our need
  And provide us with plenty of salt.

It's nice to believe that the evil they weave
  Will secure them a trip back to hell,
But better than that, wheresoever you're at,
  Is make sure you don't go there as well.

Identity Crisis

for Kentaji Brown Jackson

by Susan Jarvis Bryant

I used to think my body was all woman,
My fruitful womb refused to be dismissed.
But now I'm not so sure I'm even human—
I'm not a fully trained biologist.

I'm failing at cisgender recognition
In times when genitalia count for naught.
But I can't count, I'm not a mathematician—
The thought of naught is apt to leave me fraught.

I heard guys came from Mars and gals from Venus.
For that I make a grave apology.
I do not know my elbow from my penis
And didn't major in astronomy.

Don't ask me what the future holds in store,
My crystal balls lie busted on the floor.

Song of the Wokester

by C.B. Anderson

I'm neither he nor she—
Biology is bunk.
On water I get drunk,
And one plus one is three.

We shouldn't have to pay
For what the world provides;
Unlimited free rides,
No doubt, are here to stay.

Evacuate the jails
And let no one feel safe;
Let all the world be rife
With felons tough as nails.

Integrity is lame,
And cheating always works,
So you are in, you jerks,
The Loser Hall of Fame.

The truth is what we say
It is, and nothing more;
Unless you want a war,
Just fall in line today.

Drunk on Compassion

by Brian Yapko

How good it feels to open up your heart
And groove on how compassionate you are!
You advertise your causes on your car
And list your Facebook "likes" upon a chart.

You march in protests, always don your mask,
And quite politely call men "them" and "they,"
While voting to make decent people pay
For rancid social schemes in which you bask.

How kind to give an addict a free needle
And fund his taste for methamphetamine!
You judge him not—a new age magazine
Says not to shame the lost or make them wheedle.

Your tender heart cares so for people's pride
You buy the homeless tents in which they swelter
So they can shun a sober, Christian shelter.
You help them fail before they've even tried.

Your codependent instinct to appease
Keeps alcoholics drinking on the street.
You give them cash, ignoring how they cheat.
And where are you when they die from DT's?

You claim to love Mankind yet never will
Consider that your undiscerning "kindness"
Encourages destructiveness and blindness
And frankly helps to keep sick people ill.

Your fancies ruin lives. Address what's real
And not ideals which are no more than fiction.
Misguided kindness feeds men's dereliction.
Advancement's based on facts. Not what you feel.

So when you fawn on some crime-addled punk
While blasting those who build and who create,
Consider that it's you who nurtures hate.
Go home, my leftist friend. Because you're drunk.

.

DT: Delirium Tremens, withdrawal from alcohol, which can be fatal.

"Sound and Fury, Signifying Nothing"

—Lines On Dreadful Instagram Poetry

by S.A. Todd

A halitosis belch of steam
Spewed out in words. Ream after ream
Of cheese puff, air-stuffed offerings
Of child's-art-in-thought-bubble things
We all have pondered, never wrote,
Because to waste the time to quote
Self-evident reality
Just champions banality.

Do not mistake this righteous rant
As envy of the ignorant.
I know *why* you do what you do—
Sometimes, I like a burger too!
But when that burger tastes like dirt
You make complaint, though risking hurt
(When calling spade a spade, aloud)
From missiles hurled by baying crowd

Who think *all* criticism cruel
The purview of the snobbish fool
Who'd understand, if he but could
Ignore the trees, *adore the wood.*
To worship what it *represents*
(Mere bonus points if it makes sense)
And elevate word-salad dribbling
Stream of random stanza'd scribbling

To the heights of the profound.
Empowered, he would come around!
Nevermore would he abscond
from the inch deep and mile wide pond
Where rules the self-love muse they follow
Though their words, when tapped, ring hollow

Faulty lightbulb, twee and trite,
That heats up, sure, but sheds no light.

I should not speak unless it's nice—
Perhaps my 'Likes' will pay the price?
"Look down only if helping up"
And venerate the half-full cup.
I'll get back on my spot, and smile
Perhaps I'll like it, in a while?
Mistaking fireflies for stars
And smudge on lens for life on Mars.

Classical Camouflaged

by James Ph. Kotsybar

It begins, like all prose poems today,
with a bit of narrated diary, as though it
were a tale by Hemmingway, but more
self-conscious and less flowery.

It then proceeds to rub the reader's
nose in an unrelated past happenstance
where the tortured soul of the poet goes,
and you know it's not pretty, from a
glance.

If the audience leaves, thinking, "That's
me!" it just makes me feel sorry how
many are out there thinking: "This is
poetry," while well-trained poets don't
make a penny.

Editors prefer prose from a poet.

(This sonnet was rhymed;
I dared not show it.)

Shaving Directions

from James A. Tweedie's Prose-That's-Really-a-Sonnet Challenge

by Joseph S. Salemi

Before you shave you give your face a scrub with soapy water that's just hot enough to set your skin a-tingle. Then you rub a creamy unguent in—the perfect stuff to make a beard grow soft and oil-smooth. One minute to spread lather does the trick. That's the preparation that will soothe the razor's stroke, and help avoid a nick. Always shave twice, with a different blade. Lather again, but this time not so thickly. Pull your skin tight; make sure you don't abrade your tender flesh, and never shave too quickly. Once done, you wash and towel-dry your face until your skin's as taut as any drum. Put all the shaving things back in their place and finish with some splashes of bay rum.

> Before you shave you give your face a scrub
> With soapy water that's just hot enough
> To set your skin a-tingle. Then you rub
> A creamy unguent in—the perfect stuff
> To make a beard grow soft and oil-smooth.
> One minute to spread lather does the trick.
> That's the preparation that will soothe
> The razor's stroke, and help avoid a nick.
> Always shave twice, with a different blade.
> Lather again, but this time not so thickly.
> Pull your skin tight; make sure you don't abrade
> Your tender flesh, and never shave too quickly.
> Once done, you wash and towel-dry your face
> Until your skin's as taut as any drum.
> Put all the shaving things back in their place
> And finish with some splashes of bay rum.

(I had to use the 16-line sonnet form of George Meredith)

223

A Complaint

from James A. Tweedie's Prose-That's-Really-a-Sonnet Challenge

by K.S. Anthony

Dear Sir,

I found your challenge an offense to art, to rhyme, to reason, and to taste: a game for fools with no aesthetic sense and dilettantes whose lives are but a waste.

I demand to know your motivation and, furthermore, I think it's fair to ask you give us all some rote supplication and cancel this inane, absurdist task.

And dare I raise the question of what's next? Will "epigrams-but-rap" see Wilde spin? Perhaps a villanelle-but-over-text or other ghastly literary sin.

I hate to enter into these affrays, but here we are.

Yours truly,
KSA.

> Dear Sir, I found your challenge an offense
> To art, to rhyme, to reason, and to taste:
> A game for fools with no aesthetic sense
> And dilettantes whose lives are but a waste.
> I demand to know your motivation
> And, furthermore, I think it's fair to ask
> You give us all some rote supplication
> And cancel this inane, absurdist task.
> And dare I raise the question of what's next?
> Will "epigrams-but-rap" see Wilde spin?
> Perhaps a villanelle-but-over-text
> Or other ghastly literary sin.
> I hate to enter into these affrays,
> But here we are. Yours truly, KSA.

Mistress

by Michael Pietrack

Within those sheets, my mistress lay,
her flawless form with perfect feet.
One last embrace; I cannot stay!
I hear her heart in metered beat.

Her voice, a ballad siren song
with lyrics begging my delay.
But I've already been too long!
Within those sheets, my mistress lay.

The grandest thought one could create
was "could the wife and mistress meet?"
She'd see a villain-elle and hate
her flawless form with perfect feet.

She draws me back into the sheets.
Seductive eyes say, "Come and play,"
But I must leave this incomplete!
One last embrace; I cannot stay.

Perhaps… I'll finish this last rhyme.
One hasty end-stop short and sweet.
The chugging quatrain steams to climb!
I hear her heart in metered beat.

The writing's done… now comes the chafe.
A writer's wife airs her dismay.
The notebook, closed; my secret, safe.
Within those sheets, my mistress lay.

Free Verse

by Clive Boddy

Let us free verse from "free verse" while we can;
A pile of branches does not make a tree,
And fruit squashed on a plate does not make jam.
While words strung down a page can never be,
As eloquent as structured poetry.

Let us free verse from "free verse" while we may;
A canvas splashed with paint does not make art,
Fine pottery is more than unturned clay,
While breaking eggs alone does not bake tarts,
So, let's write verse that's organized and smart.

Let us free verse from "free verse" while we might,
Though "free verse" may win many a critics' prize
We find the meaning empty or just slight,
Disjointed words mean nothing to our eyes,
Such poetry's just prose in false disguise.

Poetry 101 Lecture
by Mary Gardner

Today we shall discuss why poems have a poor repute
(Though if one dislikes poetry, apology is moot).
Let's take four types of poems with their strong points and their faults:

Well-crafted love poems are a jewel; but most of them, near schmaltz.
Eschew the superficiality of poets callow,
Your readership wants thoughts profound, not angsty-torn and
     shallow.
Endeavor fresh perspectives or enlightenment to hone,
Nobody wants to know your pain or heartache—they've their own.

Likewise, descriptive verse engenders rolling-eyes and frown:
I see the tree. What's it to me if you tell me it's brown?
Put energy into your words! Rain rattles, sprinkles, brawls;
It washes, rinses, feeds, or flogs, but do not say it falls.
Punch up the picture in the mind, compare to what's akin,
Describe events in present tense, impel the reader in.

Haiku appears straightforward form but it is hard and trying,
Its syllables and twist of thought the simple words belying.
A complicated five-then-seven-five-again creation
Combined with subject (Nature) and a turn of observation.

It's rare to find a limerick that isn't humorous
They're easy, and like the haiku, their brevity's a plus.
Pretend-sophisticates on limericks look down their nose;
It's much the same they look on puns when they are reading prose.
But real sophisticates allow amusement to show through
They recognize its firm and rightful place as poetry true.

So, Students, please don't scrap with those who dislike poetry.
Create some good ones of your own; perhaps eventually
They'll recognize its value. If they don't, then don't persist.
Ah, there's the bell. See you tomorrow. Thank you. Class dismissed.

The Poetaster's Plight

by Kenneth L. Horne

Some think the poet's work is ease:
"Sit back and write it's such a breeze;"

But those that know will surely say
They labor hard from day to day.

They wrestle with each turn of phrase,
Constructing forms in different ways.

A quote, a comma, where to place
To space or not could bring disgrace.

You see you're writing for the ages,
Competing with so many sages.

The pressure is I hate to say
Enough to make one turn away.

Abandoning this noble task,
It's risk for me, too much to ask;

For poetry is my life's pursuit,
Without it now I can't compute.

So struggle on I'm sure I will
Until I find that word t'will fill,

Completing what I need to say
At least for one more harried day.

Decolonizing the Curriculum – Dual Scenario

on Salford University's recent treatment of the sonnet.

by Paul A. Freeman

We must decolonize our poetry
Because it's the twenty-first century,
So don't get preachy, telling me
We owe it to ourselves and our ancient codes
To read sonnets and odes,
To write limericks and rondeaux,
To revel in villanelles we compose.
I'm sure it's safe enough to say
Traditional verse has become passé;
Nobody on planet Earth can convince me
We still need rhyming and metrical poetry!

We still need rhyming and metrical poetry!
Nobody on planet Earth can convince me
Traditional verse has become passé.
I'm sure it's safe enough to say,
To revel in villanelles we compose,
To write limericks and rondeaux
To read sonnets and odes,
We owe it to ourselves and our ancient codes;
So don't get preachy, telling me
Because it's the twenty-first century,
We must decolonize our poetry.

A Note on Iambic Barktameter

I have an Australian Shepard named Sunny who loves poetry. I didn't believe it at first, but she proved it to me. She showed me her copy of Poetry magazine and said, "Look how dog-eared it is." Then she told me that her favorite poets are Percy Biscuit Shelley and Ezra Hound. And she listed her favorite poems. There's one by Christopher Marlowe called "The Passionate Australian Shepherd to His Love." Another is by John Keats. It's called "When I Have Fears That I May Cease to Bark." And then there's the classic poem by Allen Ginsberg. You know the one. And Sunny's favorite poem of all time is by Emily Dickinson. The title is "Dinner is the thing with feathers." Now I will read a poem that Sunny wrote. It's called "Iambic Barktameter."

Iambic Barktameter

by Mark F. Stone

I'm trained in poetics.
I'm schooled in aesthetics.
I'm savvy with tropes and with verses.

And what could be sweeter
than a dog who knows meter
and one who, each morning, rehearses!

Iambics are a breeze. It's hard to miss the mark.
Bark. BARK. Bark. BARK. Bark. BARK.
Bark. BARK. Bark. BARK. Bark. BARK.

Dactyls are easy. A walk in the park.
BARK. Bark. Bark.
BARK. Bark. Bark.
BARK. Bark. Bark.
BARK.

A succession of anapests gives me a spark.
Bark. Bark. BARK.
Bark. Bark. BARK.
Bark. Bark. BARK.
Bark. Bark. BARK.

See my trochees gleam and sparkle.
Barkle.
Barkle.
Barkle.
Barkle.

And a foot I think of fondly
has two stresses. It's the spondee.
BARK.
BARK.

I know my poems will take flight.
Success, I sense, is near.
I'm ready to embark upon
a stunning, new career.

My poems are not doggerel.
I'm more than just a rhymester.
They won't be selling only at
the corner five-and-dime store.

My poetry will make things happen.
It will surely sell.
My narratives must be unleashed.
I have a tale to tell.

Clowns Teach Writing Classes

by Janice Canerdy

Students' attitudes were dismal;
composition skills, abysmal!
Desperate to make things better,
teachers asked expert go-getters,
"Will you please get their attention?
What we need's an intervention,
something new-wave, fresh, progressive—
something youth will find impressive!"

"We will help you," they asserted.

"HEROES!" weary teachers blurted.
"While you fix this situation,
we'll just take a short vacation."

Dressed as clowns, with bright red noses,
"experts" told how one composes
essays. Students were attentive
to instructions so inventive:

"Slap those thoughts down. Hurry! Hurry!
Incoherent? Shucks, don't worry.
Spelling, punctuation, grammar—
Smash 'em with a great-big hammer.
Sentence structure, keep ignoring!
Writing standards are so boring.
Creativity, they smother.
Rules—I'd ban if I'd my druthers.
Pay no mind to your lame teachers.
Go play games behind the bleachers!"

Teachers soon returned expecting
with these kids they'd be connecting,
reading their descriptive writing,
in which they would be delighting.

What they found was quite confounding,
red-nosed youth in clown suits pounding
on their books with rubber hammers,
yelling, "We don't need no grammars!"

Judge Not

by C.B. Anderson

We notice, Signor Alighieri, that
You have a rather well developed bent
For taking your opponents to the mat

And showing them that in the Main Event
They will be pinned like insects to a wall
To illustrate their faults and consequent

Amercements handed out to one and all.
To place yourself upon the Judgment-Seat,
As you have done, must take a lot of gall,

And you yourself might have to face some heat
For doing so. Perhaps there's yet another pit
Reserved for those who've chosen to compete

With God, the Lord of Law and Holy Writ,
By making show of passing Justice down,
A grave imposture He does not permit.

Did Vergil never show you that? You frown,
As if you fear that I might well be right,
Or fear the caustic lake in which you'll drown.

Don't let these worries keep you up at night,
Or tremble like a stressed anemone;
Let Mercy from above allay your fright.

Make right your heart: Forgive thine enemy;
Don't play the man who fled Gethsemane.

IV. LONGER POEMS

David by Michelangelo, metallic replica of the original sculpture, 2005, Piazzale Michelangelo, Florence.

Last Letter from Florence

by Lionel Willis

A recent incident recalls the fears
Your letters have expressed: that seven years
In this art-laden place might rob me of
Whatever you once thought that you could love:
The flat I rent lies halfway up a via
Around a bend from Piazza Signoria.
A few noons back, having as usual rushed
Across the square, it came to me I'd just
Ignored the David—not the first such lapse.
The streets grow more unneighborly. Perhaps
I'm learning how to hold myself aloof:
He's not the only man without a roof.

Wasn't he sprung five centuries ago
From marble jail by Michelangelo?
And still the well-known figure stands around
Like youthful talent waiting to be found.
I too would like to find him, but the trouble's
To tell the real one from his countless doubles.
Without moving a muscle, suddenly
He's at the Palace where he used to be,
But surely at the famed Piazzale too
I've seen him stretched to get his piece of view,
And isn't that him 'neath the little dome
Where all line up and pay to find him home?
It seems that everywhere one turns he looms
In shops and alleys, restaurants and tombs,
And lilliputian legions on display
For Gullivers to hire and lead away.

The True King surely rests in none of these,
Though like an up-to-date Diogenes
He searches through the short-lived spotlit night
For that one tourist who can get him right.

No day goes by that, busied with survival,
I don't snub David like some kind of rival.
Sometimes I nod: ("I saw David again."
"How did he look?" "A bit the worse for rain.")
At last, my dreams betraying with a kiss,
Overexposure wreaks its nemesis.
Unsettled to the depths, I rise in haste
To daytime fantasies where stones play chaste
And legend clothes the onset of a man:
As monumental, ageless Peter Pan,
As the Commandant, slouching on to claim
The invitation that will spoil Juan's game,
As gleaming beauty, stalking through the street
In search of someone he seems sure he'll meet:
The severed head, perhaps, of some old boast
To bury and so lay its owner's ghost.
The sanitized imagination spins
As many roles as copies—but none wins.
Our David has been standing in the ring,
Braving all comers, stripped down to a sling,
Ready for his Goliath fate to knock
Its way out of some even tougher rock.
A lesser champ would have long since retired
Upon the forfeit purse, deadlines expired.
But David and his maker linger yet
Within the timeless moment when they met,
The form forever grasped within the stone,
The mallet poised to make the wonder known.
Now there's one David who was beautiful!
But he has never been accessible.
Another that which then the sculptor brought
To light as chip by chip he cleared his thought.
O to revisit that first nakedness
So quickly aged and wizened by the stress
Of idle talk when round the burghers came
To stare and weave their winding sheet of fame!

In fact the work of art is never done,
As days undo the dreams long nights have spun,

And ever once again through endless toil
True form seems lighted but for men to spoil,
As if they hated that which proved them blind,
Preferring blocks to Davids of the mind.

Philosophy suggests we touch the real
Where action springs, compelled by what we feel,
As in those hands I seem to clutch a hope
That some somewhere can shape where mine but grope,
Or arms extend to feed or clothe or warm
Those we should cherish since they share his form.

And now my years in Florence near a close
When we must face whatever loss now shows.
Please heed the warning issued in this letter:
The place has changed me—maybe for the better.
And if I've mended any of my flaws
David has been the most efficient cause.
For when I came I thought I knew my ends
And how to reach them. Knowledge, wealth and friends
Have withered into means to what his eyes
Forever gaze upon, the utmost prize.

I'm bringing back less luggage than I took,
Having discarded sureness book by book.
I've only change of habits to declare,
For you—and all—one gift as light as air:
No effigy with form so crudely blurred
A fig-leaf shame would be the lie preferred;
Instead a vision just beyond my reach,
An end the balance of my life may teach,
Like David's look, fixed on a distant quest,
The ever-changing light that shows us best.

Elegy for an Unremarkable Man

by Shaun C. Duncan

Poor Niel is dead. He'd been off sick since May.
Cancer, they said, as if we couldn't guess,
And, since we didn't know what words to say,
We stayed away. If pressed, we might confess
We'd turned our jellied backs to his distress,
Acting from some vain, primitive belief
It might ward off those dreams of sleeplessness
When for ourselves we lie awake in grief.
His death, when it arrived at last, was a relief.

We're left to wonder what it's like to die;
They say the drugs can wash away all pain,
But still, it must be boring to just lie
And wait, while doctors patiently explain
That slow starvation isn't inhumane
And any further care would just postpone
Your great demotion to that dark domain.
How awful it must be to die alone;
You'd hope the nurses let him hold on to his phone.

He had no faith as far as we could tell
Beyond those platitudes we all recite,
And not a word he proffered could dispel
The air of middle-class suburbanite:
Well-educated, earnest and polite
But something of an affable cliché
And quite the opposite of recondite.
Most liked him well enough but none could say
His loss aroused strong feelings in us either way.

And yet he sometimes smiled as if amused
At something we'd not understood, and in
The margins of the minutes, unperused,
His scribbled sketches spoke to discipline
And hinted at some hidden harlequin

Crouching behind the bland exterior.
Like us, he likely lived his best within
From fear we'd mock his dreams as dreary, or
Simply because he found this world inferior.

So now lost friends and fellow workers file
Into his final conference room, a space
Where emptiness is sacralized in style
Suited to governance more so than grace,
As if banality might best efface
The fear of all that black, and as we find
Our seats, a sober smile or limp embrace
For those we pass, we cannot leave behind
The mundane world and its demands upon the mind.

The celebrant is late, and so we wait
On plastic chairs and stare at tiny screens.
Then one observes this self-same real estate
Was once a place which fixed old fax machines
And such condolence wrought from pathos means
Much more to us than grieving's pantomime:
A life reduced to trite, curated scenes;
Perhaps a poem built from awkward rhyme;
And, finally, some song he said he liked one time.

Then, after sandwiches and one light beer
It's back to work as his remains are burned
And all the silly things which he held dear,
Those scraps of happiness his ennui earned
As compensation for a life adjourned
Are left beside the road. Then, once the home
Where he had lived alone has been returned
To ashes, on that land a honeycomb
Of gleaming tenements will bubble up like foam.

To stumble from the premises like this
And leave the universe without a scar,
To slip from coffee breaks to the abyss
When you've lived half your life inside your car

241

And never told another who you are,
Seems an obscenity, a tasteless joke,
Like a vacation to an abattoir,
And any cheap excuses we invoke
Will soon dissolve into the empty sky like smoke.

Yet Adam was a gardener, so they say
And, though that Paradise sounds rather nice,
It still demanded work from day to day.
And while our pride insists a higher price
Be placed upon our selfish sacrifice,
We're gifted moments pregnant with surprise,
When all around us seems to shine like ice;
We look upon the world with ancient eyes
As something small and sad inside us briefly dies

And, as we step into that ground we share
With all of Nature's gaze, we might sense one
Who waits behind us and become aware
That we have walked, backs turned against the sun,
Complaining to our shadows. Niel is done
With all that now. May he be satisfied
To leave behind those lives left unbegun
And may the rest of us forget our pride,
Knowing that better men than we have also died.

Moments from Dante's Inferno

by Paul Buchheit

Prepared to travel, if the gods allowed,
I saw the woods were dreary, dark as death.
I chose to heed a blessing there endowed,
before emerging spirits took a breath.
And that was Virgil, orator and font
of god-like wisdom. He began to speak:
"The lion, wolf, and leopard each will want
to taste your flesh before you reach the peak.
Another pathway beckons: as your guide
I'll show you spirits who await reward
as well as doomed and wretched souls denied
the entrance to the kingdom of your lord."
And then we saw, as if to sanctify
our path, a brilliant burst of golden sky.

We stood before the gates of hell. A sign
foretold the misery and dark despair,
and issued warnings blunt and saturnine:
Abandon Hope! and *Idle Souls Beware!*
A ferryman had come to shore. He turned
to take us close to Hades' borderline.
Said Virgil, "Spirits here have never earned
their destinies; through folly or design
they wasted time, embraced incompetence,
and loved themselves instead of those in need."
And as he spoke I saw the consequence
of their transgressions: worms began to feed
upon their flesh, and all the dreadful fears
of hell were flowing in their blood and tears.

We came upon the River Styx. A boat
approached, and Virgil roared, "The gods ordain
that we shall travel to the most remote
extents of hell!" Ahead, the dark terrain

243

Canto 7: The Wrathful on the Shores of the River Styx by Eric Armusik, 2020, oil on AlumaComp, 60 x 48 in. (Ericarmusik.com)

was filled with spirits stuck in oozing slime.
"I know that man!" I yelled, for there, immersed
in mud, appeared a soul who spent his time
on earth in politics, where all the worst
assaults on common people were conceived.
"It's risky here," said Virgil, "You'll survive
for now, but as a human you've achieved
the depths allowable. If you're alive
you must return." (He slyly reassured
me: "We'll continue on, you have my word.")

Along the way we faced the putrid smell
of excrement. The spirits were interred
in waste, and watched by Cérberus: all hell
was frightened by this beast—three heads assured
a view of all the flesh that he could tear
with bird-like talons. Virgil counseled: "Throw
some slime at all its heads to try to wear
him down!" But then a spirit from below
exclaimed, "We're damned because of gluttony!"
He seemed inclined to tell his tale of woe:
"I lived in self-absorbed depravity,
and paid the price. A wastrel long ago,
I'm dining now on feces like a beast!"
And so we left him to his reeking feast.

Beyond a ridge we heard the frightful sound
of women crying out, delirious
with anger. These were Furies, now unbound
from husbands, gathered with mysterious
Medusa, who had serpents in her hair
and powers magical. "You'll turn to stone,"
said Virgil with dismay. "Don't even dare
to look at her!" A Fury will dethrone
her man, my Master said. Misogyny
is first upon her plate: a man proclaims
a woman is a source of fantasy,
a charm for his indulgence. But the flames

of rightful vengeance will consume the beds
of lust as Furies rip their men to shreds.

Descending through the rocks, we heard a grunt:
the Minotaur, half-human, head of bull,
and bloody red with anger, stood in front
of boiling river water that was full
of spirits damned because of violence
on earth. And then the Centaurs came: half-horse,
half-man, with bows and arrows to dispense
their cruelty on runaways, to force
them back to Bloody River. Boiling there
were famous men: Attila, and the Great
but brutal Alexander. With a flair
for wrangling Virgil started to berate
the horsemen: "heed the gods and be our guide!"
So on the backs of Centaurs we would ride.

The next display of horror made me grieve
for spirits punished for eternity.
We saw the devils stepping up to cleave
a tongue, a neck, a groin, repeatedly.
Once healed, the spirit had its injury
renewed by demons joined in morbid rounds
of revelry. I learned the history
of spirits split in two: the common grounds
were schism and division, civil war,
and separation based on color, creed,
and other hateful reasons. Men abhor
their fellow men through arrogance or greed,
and they condemn themselves to demon knives
in punishment for all the severed lives.

And lastly, in the depths of hell, I grasped
the ghastly truth of Lucifer, the prince
of death, a triple-headed beast. I gasped
at wings and claws and teeth that might evince
a spirit's frantic plea for swift demise.
But Virgil swept me onto Satan's wing

and clambered up. Above my frightened cries
a brilliant sun appeared, a sparkling spring
enlivened us, and now, with demons gone,
I looked ahead to blessings in the dawn.

Canto 8: Covid-Priest

from The English Cantos Volume 2: StairWell

StairWell is the Poet's Purgatory, and as in HellWard where we met with contemporary challenges such as Brexit, so here in StairWell the Poet, led on by his guides Dante and Virgil, runs into another—Covid.

by James Sale

…With Dante facing a tunnel which swerved
Abruptly upwards, down which organ sounds
As from a church spilled; but we held our nerve,

Pressed on, as each step our steps unwound;
We entered into a marvelous space:
One nave, huge, high-ceilinged, a new-found land

Whose emptiness astonished—a still place,
Designed for worship but more like some crypt
In which humans might be, yet see no face.

Suddenly, as from nowhere, muffled lips
Screeched out a warning almost clear, but tart:
I heard, 'Pandemic on—feet—apart—six—

Or leave!' We shuffled unsure; Dante alert
But Virgil and I experiencing guilt—
Too close, were we? So, we were causing hurt?

Whose voice was this with its imperious lilt
And caustic accusation? And there she was,
As if up from an altar where she dwelt—

Then magicked into our presence, alas!
"I am the priest in charge—Penny Crow—
Where have you been, and have you had the vax?"

She wore the sacred vestments loose—her cope,
Cassock and tippet, grand finery of church,
So that poor Virgil shrank, felt drained of hope,

That one so high—near God—with God's own stature
From holy garments, Peter's sanction given
To be the Rock on which authority perched—

How then, without her blessing, get to heaven?
Poor Virgil—used to power, imperial-bent,
But only that type which is earthly driven;

His hopes all now above, how strange Crow's rant,
But sensing some divine rebuke within,
Taken aback by reprimand's raw cant,

How down he seemed. But what was, wasn't sin
Immortal Dante knew, who'd seen God's face.
"I come," he said, "to lead these from ruin,

To where the chapel of St Luke is placed,
Not here—where desolation's to be found—
But where at last their solace will be tasted."

Why! Reverend Crow, open-mouthed, astounded;
Did not this new-comer trespass her domain?
Was that her teeth—who else's—we heard ground?

"Excuse me, you are?" she said, annoyed, plain
Disturbed, so that why bother be polite:
Her "Jesus" enjoined not that rule or strain?

Besides, just who was this spirit of … light?
She flinched as before whom she addressed glowed,
Such that her certainties mind held took flight;

Some dubious fog-appearing danger showed;
Be careful—we saw her heart shrivel back
Into its desiccated shell of pride,

Not wanting to commit now to attack
Until identity was clarified—
Suppose this angel, bishop—what bad luck!

"I was a man once," Dante said, "but died;
Before I did, I wrote about the Popes,
Corruption in the church, and thus not shied

Away from scolding killers of Christ's hope:
That all the world might be saved, saved through Him"—
I felt it, Virgil too, a tremor's throb,

As if he had in naming of His name—
For one instant revealed—nothing stood;
Nothing could stand, for all existence lame;

The living too—all frozen in their blood
And toppled. Myself, I felt panic rise
In that recess where heart finds little good,

Wanting to cry: "Cover me—blind my eyes—
Oh, everlasting hills be my refuge!
Lest I should see the One the world despised—

And die." Now kneeling, Virgil like some stooge
To my own actions—we both stupefied—
Raised arms as if he were some thaumaturge

Who rearing mercy—the while petrified—
Perhaps might hope only grace limitless
When faith and love in us had never died

Because—as sinners in our own long chaos,
They'd never lived. And then a stillness held,
Abrupt and sudden, quiet as green moss,

Replaced the quake, unfinished and untold;
A dream we had maybe, vision to come—
When finished fully God's plan would unfold.

For now, though, we sat back, both dazed and dumb.
Above us, sensing Dante stood—advanced—
Towards the priest whose own fear—rendered numb—

Unfounded by this calm—at first, she winced
As some reflex to higher truth dismissed,
As one might to a voice heard at a séance;

Then Dante's head near close enough to kiss
Her lips, which to her suddenly loomed;
Outraged, and in recoil, she spluttered, hissed;

(The nave not big enough for all its room!)
"An epidemic's here—put on your mask—
How dare you stand so close, and so presume—"

Before her sentence closed, finished its task
However, Dante's right hand upstretched high
And pointing ceilingward he held an ankh—

From whence it came I knew not—but to the sky
Beyond the roof and steeple its ley lines
Sped on their way, awaiting their reply

Quite instantaneous: ready with His signs—
Dissolving what had seemed solid above,
We saw transparent stars in order shine,

Zodiac rotating on its wheel of love;
Already Virgil, I, were on our knees,
Now Dante fell to his, and there we shelved

Our souls in reverence. But no, not she—
Still standing, looking round witless and lost,
Unable to comprehend what all could see—

The constellation—Aries' shining ghost,
Which momentarily flickered high above,
As if a switch clicked then Aries went … lost …

Because these shepherds owed their sheep no love:
Too busy with their own right-on careers,
Too busy fiddling all their woke-riffed moves,

Too busy, busy, for souls living here—
Out from the churches, one by one, they stray,
Chewing philosophies, bleak, false and drear.

"Great God," cried Dante, "Your people can't pray—
This place—like Ripon in the north—is closed
To prayer, though they prayed on Black Death days,

And prayed when Europe's Spanish Flu was loosed;
Through each catastrophe and every war
Prayer and sacraments were diagnosed.

But you—glad tidings: Covid's what you hear!
With solemn disappointment tell the flock
For all their sakes your Archbishop's been clear:

So, slam the church door shut; and prayer, put a sock
In it—why, praying, singing songs to God
May spread disease—better God under lock.

And you, you hypocrite, pretending good,
As if you weren't glad not to tend the sheep,
Be done, abolish tedious needs for food:

Communion itself for those whom God keeps—
Beware, for 'Jesus' whom you claim to serve
Is not so mocked; and sowing's what you'll reap.

Remember Paul? Don't worry, you'll not starve,
But will—" With that, he paused, and his hand turned,
And pointing the ankh, "Get what you deserve."

Something like panic inflamed, deep-like burned
Across her face as the stars drooped to fade,
The roof grew solid, and sensing she'd be harmed,

"Stop praying," she screeched, "restrictions forbid!"
But now great Dante stood and held the while
That ankh at her face and said, "Too late."

A whisper … hissing … as of some gas-spill
Grew in intensity. "My friends, lie flat."
Instantly, we obeyed; but she stood tall.

"Hear now," cried Dante loudly, "… that estate
Saint Paul informs us of —" A sudden blast
Of fire purged through the porch's iron gate

And through the church, consuming in its path
All flesh that it encountered. We, floor-bound,
Only felt the heat above our necks, rasp—

And dare not look, eyes fixed firm to the ground.
But my mind's eye grasped all, sharp as glass is:
Fire burned upwardly, forming one massed mound—

A vaulting pillar just like one before that Moses
Saw—and which led the Israelites across
Vast deadly deserts in their hopeless darkness,

Now settled on her, intending her loss.
As some image viewed, rear-side of my head,
I saw her squirm and squeal as in flames tossed

Her being's atoms started to unthread.
Whatever's unworthy perished in this blaze;
And still beside stood Dante, unperturbed.

Then said a word, or maybe more, a phrase:
"Do you believe?" Screaming in entangled harm,
"I do! I do! I do!" nearly too late;

But soon enough; his ankh freely turned
From minatory to another aspect:
Of light that burned away the fire that burned!

253

Upon the wall of flame a new prospect
Appeared—a circle, laser cut, as one
Who burgles breaks glass—through his hand irrupts

To lift the inside latch. Now baked and done,
Her desperate hand reached out to touch his sign,
And doing so—grace works!—the pillar's gone.

Collapsing on the stone floor's hard design—
That wreck of former self, yet soul still there,
Preserved as by immortal love's strong bind

That for all perfidy still held all cure,
For those who called on that one name of Christ:
The One whose own Word He cannot forswear.

I saw him: Virgil, his own hair uprist,
As my own body trembled on the floor;
We both aware how near the Master's tryst

With her with whom He settled now the score.
I cried out, "Mercy, Lord," and hid my head,
Praying the while His Presence would pass over.

As in a sleep, and then one wakes in bed,
Sunshine is streaming through the window pane,
So sensing, I woke to morning's bright thread.

There Penny sat, re-clothed in white, and sane;
Confessing, so it seemed, to Dante beside,
Learning the alphabet of grace again:

ABCs of meaning to be Christ's bride.
In some sweet lull of time—clerestories
Allowing light to stream through reddened sides—

Dante removed himself, to join our story,
And she the while in a high psalm-like song
Continued, satisfied, re-writing history

In light of His great right against her wrong.
We moved to exit but her voice then soared
So that my heart thrilled knowing she belonged

To that heaven where heart is at the core.
How I repented hostile thoughts intended;
I wanted, yes, to stay awhile, hear more.

But go we must, and she—till singing ended
And all transformed to light in Him—must stay.
Ahead, a path from out the church wended

A new direction opposite in way
From where we'd been, now not liturgical,
More powerful, political in sway…

"THE CHAPEL OF ST. LUKE": The Royal Bournemouth Hospital where the Poet suffered his surgery for cancer has a chapel of St Luke for prayer and restoration, and the Poet extensively went there to pray.

"AND POINTING CEILINGWARD HE HELD AN ANKH": The ankh symbol—sometimes referred to as the key of life—is representative of eternal life in Ancient Egypt; its shape is a circle atop a cross.

"THE CONSTELLATION—ARIES' SHINING GHOST": Aries symbolizes the ram or sheep, who with their false priests no longer have a shepherd, and so are set to be lost.

"THIS PLACE—LIKE RIPON IN THE NORTH—IS CLOSED.": Ripon Cathedral: its crypt had been open continuously to the public for prayer for 1349 years. But it was closed during Covid-19.

"… THAT ESTATE / SAINT PAUL INFORMS US OF": 1 Corinthians 3 v 13: "each one's work will become evident; for the day will show it because it is to be revealed with fire, and the fire itself will test the quality of each one's work."

"A VAULTING PILLAR JUST LIKE ONE BEFORE THAT MOSES / SAW": Exodus 13 v 21

"UPRIST": older form of uprising

Letter from a DC Prison

by Adam Wasem

We'd seen the evidence, the ballots dropped
In loads of boxes trundled in late-night
With ballot counting claimed to have been stopped;
The windows blocked to hide observers' sight,

Suitcases dragged from under tables; more—
The laptop filled with the Bidens' dirty dealing
Dismissed as "Russian hacks;" then Big Tech whores
Would cancel anyone who mentioned "stealing."

We had to march, you see: We had no choice;
Like in those midday old-time tv shows
Wherein your son's a bully to other boys,
Or your wife is drunk since noon, right under your nose,

They made the theft so obvious, so clear
—Biden even bragged about it live!—
And said so casual, as if with no fear
That anyone who'd hear would not connive

With what they'd planned, we had to act; to vent
If nothing else, or lose our honor, our right
To be Americans, somehow. We went
To the courts, we did it right, made known our plight

And they just laughed and tossed the lawsuits out—
"No standing," said the briefs; our lying eyes
Were no match for the Democrats' political clout.
Our proof? Buried beneath an avalanche of lies.

And so we marched. We sang along the way.
I'd brought along Old Glory, held her high,
Her colors bright against the sky's dark gray.
Voice raised in song, I felt like I could fly.

The crowd stopped out in front to mill around,
Until the cops began to lob down flash-bangs
Right into the kids and grannies on the ground.
What did they think would happen? We bared our fangs

And the cops just opened up the barricade
And waved us right on through the Capitol's door.
How could we know that welcome was a charade?
Like the cop who gave that horned-hat goof a tour

Of the Senate chambers, then he got four years?
That they'd fake courtesy to lure and goad us?
Entrapment's not a word a judge wants to hear,
Or that feds played dirty, purely to railroad us.

They say we trespassed on their sacred lawn:
But that Ray Epps dude, complete with breaching crew'd
Made sure all barring gates and signs were gone.
He never got arrested. Us? We're screwed.

And, too, that megaphone guy atop the tower;
He yelled and yelled, he didn't stop to breathe or
Clear his throat: "Go in, go in! Seize power!"
The feds don't seem to care to find him either.

We know by now the fix is in, our rights
To speedy trials, impartial juries, a joke.
The left wants blood, their jackal press delights
In our ruin, while their cities go up in smoke.

Six months in lockdown, before they mentioned trials
—In isolation all but an hour a day.
No evidence, not even charges filed.
Only in prison did I learn to pray.

The guards—most black—make sure we know we're dirt;
They don't even bother to hide their glee
At knowing they've got free rein to make you hurt
For only saying "hey, I gotta pee."

We're maced routinely, beaten and ignored;
They call us "redneck," "cracker terrorist,"
And say they've fucked our wives when they get bored.
Our pleas for food, for help, just get dismissed.

I asked my cellmate—we call him "The Professor"—
Just why he marched. He did it for his grandsons,
He said, that they could call him a transgressor
As long as the nation was saved for his "little ones."

I got my dander up that he was here at all;
he should be home, not rotting in a cell.
I told the guards it was "cruel and unusual,"
Our punishment. Maybe I started to yell,

(He'd taught me a bit of law since I got nabbed)
and said our rights were being violated.
That night a gang of guards rushed in: They grabbed
My Constitution, and left, I thought: Instead

————————[REDACTED]————————
——————————————————————
——————————————————————
——————————————————————

————————[REDACTED]————————
——————————————————————
——————————————————————
——————————————————————

————————[REDACTED]————————
——————————————————————
——————————————————————
——————————————————————

I thought they'd had their fill with me, but then
————————[REDACTED]————————
——————————————————————
——————————————————————

————————[REDACTED]————————

————————[REDACTED]————————

————————[REDACTED]————————

————————[REDACTED]————————

————————[REDACTED]————————

I don't piss blood so much no more, although
I'm told the eye will never focus right.
I could protest, just wail my tale of woe,
Then think of the Founders, how some lost more than sight.

And it's hard to handle sun; months in the hole—
It puts a certain fear of freedom in you,
A fear of hope, does something to your soul:
Cuts faith to the bone, right through the flesh and sinew.

Locked away in filth and mired in sludge
I'd lost all track of how much time had passed
Until they brought my case before a judge
To justify my deeds in court at last.

"Do you feel like a patriot?" He asked,
To mock, I know. But even in my youth
I'd something in me takes it straight to task
To turn their mocking right side out with truth.

I thought about it some, and then avowed
I did; those times when just before lights out
The whole cellblock would start to sing, so loud
We'd drown those shouting asshole guards right out.

We'd sing "America the Beautiful."
I'd sing till my voice failed, failed like the light,
And then I'd listen, blind and mute, but full
Of joy, that echoed, echoed, through the night.

Give and Take

by Norma Pain

Mr. Taxman, you're a peach,
Fill your pockets we beseech.
Having money is a curse,
Please take freely from our purse.
We may catch up some time later,
Certainly your need is greater.
Money earned is ours to give,
We don't need it just to live.

Mr. Taxman, how you've grown,
From a small foundation stone.
Take from us we beg you please,
You'll get more the more you squeeze.
Take, make sure you have enough,
Save us from the need for stuff.
Go ahead, take your percent,
We don't need it for the rent.

Mr. Taxman, job well done,
Take from each and every one.
We give yearly without fail,
Such a happy fairytale.
Work for us is pure delight,
We can do it day and night.
Sleep is really overrated,
Time-consuming and outdated.

Save us, save us from our needs,
We'll survive on bread and seeds.
Take from us and take some more,
Money makes us so impure.
Fill your coffers to the brim,
Take our blood, sweat, tears; a limb.

Wanting money is so crude,
We don't need it just for food.

Struggle is our greatest pleasure,
Take our pittance for your treasure.
Take and take and take some more,
Ours the duty to endure.
We were made to work and slave,
Till we tire and hit the grave.
Take our money, go ahead,
We won't need it when we're dead.

Mr. Taxman, we're perplexed,
Mystified and rather vexed.
Youth today seem so confused,
Frankly, we are not amused.
Many of them lose their way,
Not content with meagre pay.
Choosing crime and prostitution,
Over docile contribution.

Tell us what on earth to do,
So they'll want to give to you.
Good examples we have set,
Giving much more than we get.
Certainly they're well and able,
Working jobs under the table,
But their taxes they neglect,
Showing utmost disrespect.

Crime is getting worse and worse,
How this must affect your purse.
Judges and the lawyers too,
Suffering along with you.
People everywhere complaining,
That their taxes are too draining.
Wages way behind inflation,
Grow-ops seen as their salvation.

Mr. Taxman, this won't do,
Everyone is mad at you.
But we know you do your best,
May we quietly suggest...
Increase taxes even more.
Test how much we can endure.
Paying taxes gives us grace,
Puts a smile upon our face.

Makes us humble, teaches too,
How we may bow down to you.
Keep us poor and on our knees,
Do not let us prosper please.
Character is built on need,
Corruption the result of greed.
Ruthlessness should be your goal,
Mr. Taxman... take our soul.

Lilies After a Storm by Jeffrey Vaughn, 2019, oil and acrylic on canvas, 24 x 24 in. Gallery representation: George Billis Gallery, 1700 Post Road, Fairfield, CT. (Jeffreyvaughn.com)

V. ESSAYS

What Makes a Good Haiku?

by Margaret Coats

The required 5-7-5 syllable form alone does not make a haiku. A good haiku

- presents an observation of nature, or of human activities in nature
- uses present tense ("goes" or "going," not "went" or "has gone")
- has a seasonal word or image, known in Japanese as a "kigo"
- has two parts or two images or two aspects
- offers an intriguing insight that arises from interaction of the two parts

Below are examples of good haiku, chosen from runners-up and other entries in 2021. They fulfill *all* the above haiku requirements, but are grouped to allow for easy discussion of one requirement at a time, in the paragraph that follows each group.

The 17 Syllables in English

These first four haiku show how poets writing in English can naturalize the required Japanese syllabic form by using features of English poetry, including rhythm, rhyme, and alliteration. These things are neither required nor specially favored in this competition. However, they add beauty to the poem and demonstrate the poet's skill with language.

> Dark branches stripped bare
> cold and sad, quite unaware
> stirrings down below
>
> —Linette Eloff

266

Snow falls through the night
Dressing farm and field in white—
Dazzling dawn in sight!

—Martin Rizley

one lone(ly) mallard
ignored by his own echo
quacks again, hoping

—James Ripley

Curious concert—
crickets croon to a cornfield
of indifferent ears

—Martin Elster

Linette Eloff captures late winter in three lines appropriately rhymed
and metered. The third line, with the same number of syllables as the
first, has more word accents or stresses. It thus has more of the deep
"stirrings" it mentions—and it breaks away from the "bare"/
"unaware" rhyme and tone of the other lines. Contrast Martin Rizley's
winter haiku, which exhibits regular English rhythm, rhyme, and
alliteration in all three lines. These suit the exuberant tone of his poem.
James Ripley uses another tactic. His parentheses in the word
"lone(ly)" emphasize the meaning he can add to his first line with the
required fifth syllable. The quacking mallard is both "lone" (solitary)
and "lonely" (forlorn). Martin Elster makes every syllable count,
accompanying his farm concert with both alliteration from the noisy
crickets, and a pun on the indifferent ears of corn in the audience.

Artistry of the Present Tense

end of the summer—
the calm surface of a lake
absorbs the twilight.

—Marek Kozubek

Looming laden clouds
Blanket Bombay's bustling streets
And storms paint the sky

—Stuti Sinha

taste of morning tea
the delicate ray of sun
through an icicle

—Daniela Misso

The group above shows varied artistry employing the required present tense. Marek Kozubek uses a single present tense verb ("absorbs") to describe minimal action, but it manages to fill his noiseless scene with light and color. Stuti Sinha's poem brims with action: present tense verbs "blanket" and "paint," present participles "looming" and "bustling," along with the past participle "laden," acceptable in haiku because used as an adjective. These combine to build up a picture of increasingly wild weather over a busy city. In Daniela Misso's haiku, there are no verbs at all. Present tense is presumed in the action of a human observer who notices the sunlit icicle while sipping tea.

The Two-Part Haiku

black skyscrapers scratch
at something beyond the gray
as white flakes drift down

—Spencer Green

As winter draws near
Fabulous floral worlds bloom
The solace of books

—Mia P. Solomonides

Wisteria blooms
Along a sidewalk café
Coffee in the air

—Ravi Kivan

watermelon patch
I let the weathered scarecrow
try on my straw hat

—Darrell Lindsey

Like new fallen snow
Seabirds rest then I approach
White riot of flight

—Mike Bryant

A haiku should have two parts or two images or two aspects. The two things contrast or combine creatively to produce the poem's overall effect. Spencer Green's skyscrapers do not wait passively for snow, but actively scratch it out of the gray sky. Mia Solomonides teases readers with a flagrantly impossible winter scene—then explains that it exists in the books one can comfortably read indoors on a cold day. Ravi Kivan makes clever use of the related words "café" (a place) and "coffee" (a beverage served in such a place) to appeal to the two senses of sight and taste. In all three poems, Part One is the first two lines, and Part Two the final line. This is usual among haiku, but not universal. Darrell Lindsey sets the scene in his first line, then enters and alters it in the remaining two lines. Mike Bryant's poem is a very unusual haiku that divides exactly in the middle, where the quiet scene moves to action. His ninth syllable, the word "then," is something like a Japanese kireji or "cutting word," but such words have functions in Japanese that are unfamiliar in the English language. Poets writing in English shouldn't save a syllable to slice lines, but simply make sure that each haiku has two elements that can interact in an interesting way.

The Intriguing Insight

How can haiku demand an original insight in every poem? Remember, first of all, that this most difficult requirement is simply a special perception from the poet's own carefully observed scene.

Boughs froth with new blooms
when the monsoon rain sweeps through
trees toss their bouquets

—Rachel Nel

How short is freedom
gained by the cherry blossom
released from the branch

—Germain Droogenbroodt

Falling August stars
The sky is full of beauty
So many wishes

—Vita

All three of these poems view something beautiful falling. Rachel Nel
sees monsoon rain sweeping frothy blooms from boughs; she thinks of
a bride tossing her bouquet to others as the wedding celebration ends.
Good thought—and no more is needed. The poem is done, and the
poet doesn't have to picture anyone catching soggy flowers. The more
philosophical Germain Droogenbroodt reflects on the distance
between branch and ground when a cherry blossom falls. To him, this
brings thoughts of short-lived freedom. Again, enough insight for an
excellent haiku, expressed in terms of the bloom being released from
the prison of the branch. Vita sees stars fall during summer meteor
showers. The additional light and motion brighten and beautify the
already starry sky—and the observer gains hope for many wishes
fulfilled, in accord with the proverb, "to wish upon a falling star."

Quality Alone Cannot Qualify

What is a Haiku?
Beautiful words . . . not many
Alas! Not these words

—Norma Pain

This clever poem in haiku form is good and true and beautiful, but it is
not a haiku. If you don't know why not, please read over the Examples
and Explanation again. Looking forward to your haiku!

Daedalus and Icarus by Anthony van Dyck (1599–1641), circa 1615-1625, oil on canvas, 45.4 x 34 in.

Creativity, Originality, and Eccentricity

by Joseph S. Salemi

I don't know why it should be so, but I have a propensity to attract the attention of eccentric persons. Three times, at three separate academic conferences, I have been cornered by earnest little nerds who insisted on telling me their crackpot theory of who *really* wrote Shakespeare's plays. I happen to think that all anti-Stratfordians are obtuse cranks with a deficient sense of Elizabethan literature, and I made that view very clear to each of these three tormentors. But it didn't help. In every case, they wouldn't let me go until I had heard all the mind-numbing twists of their scenarios of forgery and conspiracy.

Then there was the nut at *MLA* who, having found out that I am a poet, insisted on outlining his scheme for reconciling free verse and metrical verse by using snippets of each as random glosses on the other. He planned to start with Milton, interlarding every ten lines of *Paradise Lost* with passages from Ginsberg's *Howl*. He wanted to know if I would be interested in collaborating with him on the project. I tried to be polite and not laugh in his face. Luckily the MLA conference is a big operation, so I managed to get lost in the crowds.

In fact, rampant eccentricity is one of the main reasons I stopped attending poetry readings. It was nice to meet one's friends and fellow poets, but there was no way to avoid the garrulous old lady who wanted you to assess her one hundred haiku on her pet cat; or the ex-mental patient wearing a rope for a belt; or the grim environmentalist with an interminable epic on pollution, badgering you to locate a publisher for it. Then there were the dry drunks, the *enragés*, the fag-hags, and the feminists. The last straw for me was the reading at which a performance-poet tossed confetti in the air as he half-sung and half-chanted his opaque work. "*Basta*," I told myself, "I don't need this swiving idiocy."

Later on my mentor, Alfred Dorn, tried to convince me to give poetry readings another shot. His basic argument was this: "We have to tolerate the weak sisters." I replied "Alfred, you're a much more patient man than I am."

One of the attitudinal problems of the present day is the confusion of eccentricity, creativity, and originality. They are not the same thing at all, despite what kindergarten teachers may tell you. They are separate and often completely independent of each other. Let's consider each in turn.

Creativity is an interior wellspring of dynamism that impels one to rearrange pre-existent reality (like matter or language) into something beautiful. It's an itch to make, to produce, to harmonize disparate elements into a formal whole. I may feel an urge to build a piece of furniture according to some design in my thoughts, or to bind an old book in an attractive cover, or to put together a sonnet by employing a new conceit or image. To use a rare and antique word, creativity is *daedal*. The term is from the Greek *daidaleos*, which means "cunningly or curiously wrought." (The name of the mythical Greek artisan Daedalus is based on this word.) Creativity is daedal because it involves two things: an urge to work, and a concomitant desire to make the product of that work as perfect and as embellished as possible. Truly creative people don't just "let it all hang out," as the stupid 60s cliché has it. They are meticulous and picky and fussy. They work hard to produce something harmonious and aesthetically satisfying, and which shows off their *virtù*. That's what it means to be daedal.

Originality is another thing altogether. Originality is what might be called one's "voice" or "signature" or "fingerprint." As the act of creation goes on, aspects of one's idiosyncratic personal identity, habits, and attitudes become inextricably embedded in the emerging product. For example, it is said that metallurgists can analyze an unmixed sample of gold and tell you, by its profile of trace elements, in exactly what part of the world the gold was mined. The same is true for works of art. They manifest in their very structure and texture the personal source from which they took life. That is what is correctly meant by "originality." The work of art shows signs of its origin. Originality does *not* mean, as many persons think, the process of coming up with something totally new and unheard-of. Originality is the penumbra of unique personal style that surrounds creativity's products.

Now let's look at the cuckoo in the nest: *eccentricity*. Eccentricity is neither creative nor original. As its etymology suggests, it refers to being "off-center," like the misplaced axle of a wheel. An eccentric is one who acts in an *outré* manner, behaving in ways that simply do not comport with ordinary conventional expectations. Let me emphasize that this does not allude to issues of taste or opinion. Eating tripe and onions every night or being a member of the Flat Earth Society doesn't necessarily make you an eccentric. Eccentricity means being erratic and unpredictable in a way that is somewhat disturbing or unsettling to others. Someone whose house is filled with stray cats is an eccentric. Or who refuses to remove his hat at the dinner table. Or who wears a red-and-white checkered suit in public. Or who insists on playing a trombone at 4 a.m. There's a kind of pathetic haplessness about eccentrics, as if they were mental defectives, or silly drama-queens, or just ornery misfits. The normal response of most people to eccentricity is not so much anger as exasperation.

In the arts, eccentricity is always disastrous. It leads persons to do things that are utterly without aesthetic justification or rationale. A lot of the silly, off-the-wall craziness that goes on in the mainstream arts today is solely the result of eccentricity, and nothing else. There is no "creativity" involved therein. Eccentricity in the arts is just a puerile need to be obstreperous or shocking, out of allegiance to some *esprit contrariant*. Much of what is called "performance" art, or "conceptual" art, or "aleatory" art is not a manifestation of creative energy or originality. It is just bizarre eccentricity, not far removed from the mental state of the Collyer brothers, or Hetty Green, or the elderly Howard Hughes. The only major difference is that the artists posture in public, and sometimes manage to snag grant money.

I can already hear the chorus: *Blake was an eccentric! Whitman was an eccentric!* Well, that's simply untrue. Examine the life and work habits of either man. Blake had a volcanic creativity that he channeled into the most complex and rigorous forms. Not only did he elaborate an intricate private mythology, he also invented his own unique method of engraving and printing books. That is profoundly daedal, as all true creativity must be. Just because Blake could be a bit strange and unconventional has no bearing whatsoever on the rigorous way in which he exercised his immense talent. As for Whitman, the man who spent decades in painstaking revision of edition after edition of *Leaves of Grass* is an example of pure daedal creativity.

As I have argued frequently in the past, a great many contemporary problems are due to the misconceptions and distortions of Deweyite ideology in our schools. That is certainly the case in regard to the confusion of creativity, originality, and eccentricity. Because of their reflexive tendency to favor impulse and feeling over restraint and structure, Deweyites will always reward spontaneity and immediacy in students. It's a matter of principle with them. *Don't give me an argument over this—I'm a teacher and I have seen it up close!* A child who hands in a slovenly, fingerpainted mess will get a big gold star for "energy" and "vitality," while another child who hands in a carefully delineated picture will be told that it is "insufficiently exciting," or "too controlled." Teachers with attitudes like that are criminals, and murderers of true creativity. They deserve to rot in hell.

As a result of these distortions, there is a major difference between the way we look at art and the way our ancestors did. Whereas in the past artistic creativity was assumed to be governed by order, restraint, and patterned symmetry, today most people unconsciously assume that the reverse is true—namely, that artistic creativity is by its nature chaotic, wild, unrestrained, and freaky. What was once the purview of Apollo is now considered the realm of Dionysos. If you don't think this is an important and far-reaching change, think harder. An aesthetic history of the last century could be written taking the collapse of Apollonian criteria as the ultimate source of all changes and style shifts.

Dionysos is a great god, as Pentheus learned in the most savage manner. All honor to him. But he is not the god of poetry and the other arts. We poets are beholden to the rational order and chaste harmony of the Delian deity, whose cold restraint and measured rhythms are a signature of our labors. When Apollo is the guardian of the arts, you get Mozart and Bach. Make Dionysos the ruler of the arts, and you get Elvis Presley and Mick Jagger.

Don't be drunk and disorderly. Be daedal.

Classical Poetry and the Martial Ethos

by Andrew Benson Brown

The Heroic Age

Towards the end of "Egil's Saga," one of the masterpieces of Icelandic literature, the eponymous hero composes a verse to eulogize a fallen friend:

> Their numbers are dwindling, the famous
> warriors who met with weapons
> and spread gifts like the gold of day.
> Where will I find generous men,
> who beyond the sea that, nailed with islands,
> girds the earth, showered snows of silver
> on to my hands where hawks perch,
> in return for my words of praise?

Egil is remembering the deeds of his loyal friend Arinbjorn, who had been killed in battle fighting a son of Egil's mortal enemy, King Eric Blood-Axe of Norway. But more than a simple commemorative verse, Egil expands his theme to express nostalgia for the Viking lifestyle that was already beginning to pass into memory in his lifetime. Iceland's peaceful transition to Christianity in the year 1000 ensured that the religion and customs of the Vikings would gradually vanish, rather than be violently suppressed as it was in other places. This diplomatic coexistence facilitated the island's vibrant storytelling culture to give rise to a unique manuscript tradition, allowing us to glimpse the lost values of a people who have captured the imagination of all future generations.

Egil Skallagrimson, who happens to be medieval Iceland's greatest poet, was also one of the great warriors of the Viking Age. While such a dual role might seem strange or incongruous today, this was not unusual in Scandinavian culture. On the contrary, the connection between poetry and the martial ethos was a vital one. The ecstatic composition of verse was seen as being akin to the manic state of the "berserker" in battle. This perception was reflected in worship of the

More Are with Us by Mark Keathley, oil on canvas, 2020, 60 x 48 in. ("the Art of Mark Keathley" on Facebook; Mark Keathley on Instagram)

god Odin, patron of both poets and warriors. The former's inspiration served to complement and commemorate the frenzied deeds of the latter. Given that these roles could co-exist in the same person, as with Egil, this sometimes amounted to boasting of one's own accomplishments, past or prospective. Other functions relevant to the moment might include sending vengeful messages to one's political enemies, warning friends of treachery, or encouraging bravery. Egil himself apparently composed his first verses at a feast when he was only three years old (though as large and strong as a boy of six or seven), reciting a drinking song and a paean of gratitude for the host.

Skaldic verse as exemplified by the above stanza was popular in Scandinavian court culture of the 10th and 11th centuries, and poets held positions of authority comparable to the respect scientists are accorded in our own society. At the beginning of "Egil's Saga," we are given the following description of Harald Fairhair's court, the father of Eric Blood-Axe and the first King of Norway: "Of all his followers, the king held his poets in highest regard, and let them sit on the bench opposite his high seat." Included in this list of honorees are the colorfully named "Audun the Uninspired," "Thorbjorn Raven," "Olvir Hump," and "Bard the White," also known as "Bard the Strong." The epithets alone tell us a great deal about a culture where a father would allot his son a predetermined destiny by naming him "Bard" and abandon him to live at court. These poets accompany King Harald on his expedition of Norwegian conquest, fighting alongside the berserkers. Those who live amass great wealth, and those who die achieve immortal glory.

After being introduced to these poets, we meet Egil. Stubborn, arrogant, and brooding, we follow his life story as his brutal but unbending sense of justice leads him to take revenge for personal sleights and perceived treachery. His intergenerational feud with the Norwegian royal family brings him fame and misfortune alike. Throughout the saga, eight-line stanzaic verses are integrated into the prose to express emotions, deepen characterization, and emphasize that the field of conflict is as much about verbal acrobatics as it is clashing swords. There are three longer poems as well. In one chapter when Egil is about to be executed by Eric Blood-Axe, he recites a twenty-stanza ode in praise of the king and is allowed to leave unmolested. The scene shows how Egil's temperamental nature is the source of both his spontaneous poetic recitation and the violent behavior that gets him into so much trouble: the two vocations interpenetrate and inflate his greatness in each arena. Were he just a good poet or a good warrior he would not only be seen as a lesser practitioner in both categories, but would never have even survived to old age. In the end he retires to Iceland, unable to reconcile his obstinate ways and semi-outlaw status with a changing Norwegian society.

"Egil's Saga" is generally believed to have been written by Snorri Sturluson, Egil's descendant and the father of Icelandic literature. Snorri was also a poet, and used many of his own compositions in writing the "Háttatal," the final section of the Prose Edda that functions as a poetry textbook. As Iceland's most famous lawspeaker, twice-elected to that nation's highest political office, he approximated Shelley's ideal of the Poet as Legislator of the World—and an acknowledged one, to boot—until being assassinated by his political enemies.

Many of the sagas of Icelanders feature poetry as integral to the story and characters. In addition to describing swaggering poet-warriors like Egil, four sagas feature love poets as their main protagonists. Lest one think that Hallfred the Troublesome Poet or Gunnlaug Serpent-tongue are tranquil troubadour-types, however, the plots of these sagas usually involve rival versifiers spitting metaphorical acid at one another while vying for the same woman. Even in Old Norse romantic poetry, the martial ethos prevailed.

Versifying Valor

While the sagas of Icelanders reflect the particularities of Viking culture, they also embody the general mores of a brutal pre-industrial world where poetry and violence were often intermingled. The *Iliad* and the *Bhagavad Gita* both portray societies where ethics is governed by honor, although Krishna counsels Arjuna to uphold a sense of duty rooted in "selfless action" that Achilles (if not Hector) would have found baffling.

The ecstatic Viking poet-warrior, too, had his parallels in other times and places. The parallel Greek notion of the poet receiving divine inspiration from the muse comes to mind, and while actual poetic composition involves at least as much perspiration as inspiration, such perceptions are undeniably useful. Many of the greatest writers of ancient Greece and Rome eschewed the modern obligation to specialize. Sophocles was elected as a general based on the public esteem for his new play "Antigone," and shortly afterwards he assisted Pericles in suppressing a rebellion on the island of Samos. Horace fought on the losing side at the Battle of Philippi, where (so he tells us in one of odes) he threw away his shield and ran, only to be veiled in mist by Mercury so that he could live to write poetic compositions. While there is no direct evidence for it, I find it hard to believe that the Spartan lyric poet Alcman was not raised in the manner Plutarch describes as the standard rigorous upbringing for a boy in that society. Aeschylus's gravestone epitaph spoke only of his "noble prowess" in "the grove of Marathon," and mentioned nothing of his verse dramas. His "Oresteia" trilogy, like "Egil's Saga," is also about a world transitioning to a legal system where honor-bound revenge-killings no longer have a place.

Fast-forward to Medieval Europe and we find another figure worthy of Egil: Taillefer, a minstrel at the Norman court of William the Conqueror. At the Battle of Hastings, Taillefer recited "The Song of Roland" on the front lines to boost morale and taunt the enemy. He then singlehandedly led a charge against the English army that supposedly turned the tide of the conflict. So if you ever encounter the test question, "Why is modern England the way it is?" you can answer: "Because of Taillefer." The professor will probably give you failing marks, but you will not be wrong. I defer here to the German poet Ludwig Uhland's description of the scene:

So Taillefer rode on before the glittering Norman line
Upon his stately steed, and waved a sword of temper fine;
Above the embattled plain his song rang all the tumult o'er–
Of Roland's knightly deeds he sang and many a hero more.

And as the noble song of old with tempest-might swelled out,
The banners waved and knights pressed on with war-cry and with
  shout;
And every heart among the host throbbed prouder still and higher,
And still through all sang Taillefer, and blew the battle-fire.

281

Then forward, lance in rest, against the waiting foe he dashed,
And at the shock an English knight from out the saddle crashed;
Anon he swung his sword and struck a grim and grisly blow,
And on the ground beneath his feet an English knight lay low.

The Norman host his prowess saw, and followed him full fain;
With joyful shouts and clang of shields the whole field rang again,
And shrill and fast the arrows sped, and swords made merry play
Until at last King Harold fell, his stubborn carles gave way.

According to most accounts the enemy troops overwhelmed Taillefer, who was apparently still singing the "Chanson de Roland" while killing at least five English soldiers. In Uhland's ballad, though, he survives to drink a victory toast with William.

Several later poets in the English tradition combined their roles with that of soldier. Chaucer fought in the Hundred Years' War, and was captured and ransomed. Henry Howard, Earl of Surrey, who helped Thomas Wyatt introduce the sonnet into English literature, was another warrior whose quarrelsome temper got him into trouble. Despite advice to seek "the quiet mind; / The equal friend; no grudge, no strife;" and other such peaceable exhortations in one of his most famous poems, Surrey had a hard time keeping boon companions. Unlike Egil's brush with Eric Blood-Axe, his versifying talents did not save him from being beheaded by Henry VIII. Another great sonneteer of the Tudor period, Sir Philip Sidney, was shot in the thigh while fighting the Spanish and died of gangrene a month later. Lord Byron famously joined the Greek struggle for independence from the Ottomans, but was laid low by fever while leading a campaign.

In general then, it would seem that personally embodying the martial ethos does not bode well for bards. Egil was a lucky case. More often, poets of the modern age wrote about war rather than practicing it themselves. As late as the 19th century, Victorian poets still celebrated the heroic spirit that had led them to become masters of the world. Tennyson, the representative poet of the age, frequently addressed questions of empire in his poems. "The Charge of the Light Brigade" is one of the great commemorative poems in British history. It paid tribute to a shocking military disaster during the Crimean War, and its immortal lines, "Theirs not to reason why / Theirs but to do and die," have long outlasted any public memory of the event itself. Equally famous are the closing lines of "Ulysses," which have been seen as encapsulating the entire Victorian worldview:

> We are not now that strength which in old days
> Moved earth and heaven, that which we are, we are;
> One equal temper of heroic hearts,
> Made weak by time and fate, but strong in will
> To strive, to seek, to find, and not to yield.

Queen Victoria so admired Tennyson's work that in 1884 she named him Baron Tennyson. It was the first time someone has been raised into the nobility on the basis of literary merit alone.

The other best-known example of our theme from this period is Thomas Babington Macaulay's collection, *Lays of Ancient Rome*—one of the last successful poetic expressions of pure martial valor and nobility. Better remembered today as a historian, Macaulay's ballads about the early Roman republic were hugely popular upon their initial publication and became mandatory reading in public schools for over a century. Winston Churchill won a student prize for memorizing them as a teenager. Surprisingly, there are still a few places where this cultural practice lives on. Highlands Latin, a private Christian school in Louisville, Kentucky, has something called The Horatius Society. Each year its 6th graders, along with homeschoolers participating in its online academy, can gain admission to this exclusive club by reciting from memory all 560 lines of "Horatius at the Bridge," which contains the once-famous stanza:

> Then out spake brave Horatius,
> The Captain of the Gate:
> "To every man upon this earth
> Death cometh soon or late.
> And how can man die better
> Than facing fearful odds,
> For the ashes of his fathers,
> And the temples of his Gods."

One can even watch a list of charming YouTube videos that record these children's recitations (which, depending on speed of delivery, take 15 to 20 minutes). Some are quite theatrical, full of dramatic gesticulations. One orator was only nine years old at the time of participating. Budding bards who complete this impressive feat are awarded a certificate in a public ceremony and receive an engraved bronze medal featuring an armor-clad Horatius standing guard in front of the Sublician bridge. Highlands Latin School is proof that children can still obtain a real education today if their parents know where to look. Churchill would be proud of these young Virgilians.

An Age of Wimps

Aside from occasional traditionalists who homeschool their children or send them to private religious academies, such educational programs are long a thing of the past. Poetry stopped celebrating martial valor at the outbreak of the First World War. It is notable that, unlike in the idealizing Victorian Age, the best poets of this period were all soldiers thoroughly disillusioned with their drafted vocation. Wilfred Owen's innovations in jarring pararhyme and jerky iambic meter created a haunting verisimilitude to being gassed or meeting dead soldiers in the underworld. Given the horrors of mechanized warfare it is understandable that he would focus on the existential meaninglessness of it all, especially when his own personal tragedy is weighed in the balance. One might speak of Owen's final year of life as his *annus horribilis:* writing all of his poems while recuperating in a hospital, then returning to the front to be killed a week before the Armistice.

The last notable poem on our subject (in English at least) is probably Randall Jarrell's "The Death of the Ball Turret Gunner":

> From my mother's sleep I fell into the State,
> And I hunched in its belly till my wet fur froze.
> Six miles from earth, loosed from its dream of life,
> I woke to black flak and the nightmare fighters.
> When I died they washed me out of the turret with a hose.

The image of the gunner "hunched upside-down in his little sphere ... like the fetus in the womb," as Jarrell wrote in an explanatory note to the poem, is a powerful one, and I must confess that this is my favorite free-verse poem. Nevertheless, its negative view of institutionalized violence has served as the swan song for martial poetry. Since Jarrell, no successful poet has written about war.

And yet the popularity of shows like HBO's "Band of Brothers" or the recent film "The Outpost," about the Medal of Honor recipients at the Battle of Kamdesh, proves that war's horror is not unmixed with its glory. Even though the former experience may predominate today (and always did, really), there are still those who occasionally bask in the latter. "The Outpost" managed to convey both qualities well in a way that is not ironic or negative like the best films about Vietnam or Iraq.

So, given the fair number of decent war films, one might expect to see a comparable revival in poetry that, if not glorifying war, at least highlights its nobility in equal measure with its familiar nightmarish traits. But one has not seen this. Why?

The answer is partly due to aesthetic, and partly cultural, reasons. Free verse is not particularly suited to telling a story. When bent to the narrative mode the result is rambling and tedious, as Tim Miller's civil war epic, "To the House of the Sun," demonstrates. Nor does one ever seem to encounter free verse poems that praise a subject or treat a theme in a positive way—unless that subject is the writer. Irony, emotional negativity, and narcissism predominate.

If free verse seems the wrong direction to look towards in launching an aesthetic counter-revolution, the free verse poet is even more of a dead end. A wimp, a nerd, a "victim" whining over imaginary oppressions, the free verse poet is the Anti-Egil: more of a partial human than a martial one. In place of a coherent ethos, one encounters the bathos of identity politics, with its never-ending redefinitions of categories. From the sublime heights of classical poetry we have lapsed into the trivial and unintentionally ridiculous. In place of genuine passion and excitement, we are treated to confessions of mental illness and childish exhortations to just "be nice." Where Egil endured the Ragnarok-like environment of remote Iceland, Instapoet Rupi Kaur barely survives a blip in her Internet service.

As long as the diversity bureaucracy is ascendant, with its domination of publishing venues, prize boards, and educational institutions, it will promote proletarian literature that is "safe," "accepting"—and sterilized of anything real. In such a climate of infantile vocabularies and socialist agendas, high quality formal poetry has little chance of becoming popular, whatever the subject or theme. To circumvent mainstream degeneracy, alternative routes of cultural transmission must continue to be paved. While this may seem like an unrealistic goal, it is more a question of maintaining a momentum that has already begun. As legacy media continues to discredit itself by making a bedfellow of radicalism, younger outlets like *The Daily Wire* and *The Epoch Times* are slowly gaining traction.

Attitude is everything. It is naïve to think that the struggle against Western decline is anything less than a war. We cannot, like the Viking poet-warriors of old, "go to the dueling-place" and swing our swords like "a serpent inflicting wounds," "silence troublemakers with iron" to "feed eagle flesh," be "makers of blood-waves for ravens," or "wet our stout branches" with "the war-goddess's wound-sea." In the age of law and officialdom, we must remain nonviolent. But this does not mean we should cultivate a posture of passive conciliation and compromise. There seems to be no longer enough common ground for mutual understanding, and the opposition grows more aggressive with every new concession made. As Egil warned, "No cuckoo will alight knowing / that the squawking eagle prowls." For our purposes, one might choose to interpret this as: "be wary of attending poetry workshops where you are invited to 'have a conversation.'" Stand up to the bullies and liars tearing down America. And where possible, couch any violent threats in the enigmatic diction of Old Norse kennings to maintain plausible deniability.

NOTES

1. Bernard Scudder's 2005 translation of Egil's eulogy for Arinbjorn, included above, does not preserve the six-syllable structure, use of regular alliteration, or mix of full rhymes with half-rhymes that is typical of the eight-line "dróttkvætt" (or "court meter") stanza. By way of comparison, here is W.C. Green's 1893 translation that, while archaic, gives more of a sense of what it would have been like in Old Norse. Note the alternation of two alliterative sounds in odd lines with one sound at the beginning of even lines:

Mead-givers, glorious men,
Gold-spending warrior wights
Are spent and gone. Where seek
Such lavish donors now?
Erewhile, beyond the sea,
Earth's islet-studded belt,
Such on my high hawk-perch
Hailed down the silver shower.

2. The passage from Ludwig Uhland's ballad "Taillefer" was translated by A.I. du Pont Coleman. It is the only English translation I am aware of.

Fortitude by Neilson Carlin, 2010, oil on canvas, 40 x 30 in.
(Neilsoncarlin.com)

A Call for Secession

by Adam Sedia

The fine arts currently lie atrophied in utter decline and degradation. Poetry is no exception. Ever since the advent of modernism in the decades leading up to the First World War, traditional aesthetic, which features realism in narrative and depiction and adherence to form, structure, and harmony, yielded completely to the modernist aesthetic, characterized by noncontextual imagery and avoidance of any structural formalities.

In poetry, modernism took the form of "free verse"—the abandonment of rhyme, meter, and form—and the abandonment of narrative in favor of pure description. In adopting this style, early modernist poets such as Ezra Pound and T.S. Eliot consciously followed the path blazed by Cubism in the visual arts, which deconstructed the visual image by presenting it from different perspectives at once, leaving it up to the viewer to conceive the full image. Using language instead of images, modernist poets presented series of images, leaving ultimate interpretation to each individual reader. Classical music, too, experienced a parallel revolution at the same time, with the adoption of the twelve-tone technique that consciously avoided any tonal center.

Despite some notable exceptions—Robert Frost, Edna St. Vincent Millay, and Richard Wilbur in the United States and Walter de la Mare and John Betjeman in the United Kingdom, among others— modernism remained the overwhelmingly dominant aesthetic in poetry. And so it has remained with the other arts, as well.

The modernist aesthetic is at its core nihilistic. It denies objective reality, and therefore meaning. Without meaning, no objective standard for beauty exists—hence form and harmony become meaningless, or "tools of oppression." And without meaning, art becomes less an expression than an elicitation of a reaction; the artist's task is to throw something out and let each individual in the audience try to make sense of it. And none of them will necessarily have the wrong answer. Thus, art devolves into the realm of radical subjectivity.

With such nihilism at its core, the modernist aesthetic had as its chief virtue only the shock of its novelty. It broke all the traditional rules. It was revolutionary, and like every revolution, it had to maintain its momentum lest its energy flag and it perish from inertia. Rushing feverishly to "break new ground," modernist art embarked on a perpetual quest for the new. Inevitably, this led to pushing boundaries of taste and even decency. Almost immediately, modernism devolved into "found art" such as Duchamp's famous urinal and in a few decades it would result in Basquiat's street graffiti and Serrano's bodily fluids being exhibited as high art.

Poetry devolved in a similar fashion, though not quite as spectacularly. A century after modernism's first stirrings as Imagism, poetry devolved into lifeless lists such as Elizabeth Alexander's 2009 inaugural poem or casual prose chats split into lines as in the works of Billy Collins. But poetry has mostly followed academic trends, fetishizing racial, gender, and sexual identities as the essence of being. Nearly every contemporary mainstream poet has fallen into this vice, and the identity-pushing has only accelerated with the ascendance of critical theory.

Thus the current state of the arts—a state of decades-long atrophy. What poses as avant-garde is actually reactionary. The aesthetic ideals that first materialized around the First World War remain unchanged: abstraction in the visual arts, atonality in music, free verse in poetry. Stylistic details may vary, but the language remains unchanging and monolithic. For the past six decades, dominance of the modernist aesthetic over the art world has been unquestioned. Only those artists, poets, and composers who operate within its framework receive the prestigious prizes, the lucrative commissions, the media attention.

And woe to the artist who dares deviate from this orthodoxy! At best, he will be condemned to work "outside the mainstream," with only a "cult" following. Those who do garner attention are labeled as some form of reactionary, likely compared with the Nazis—a favorite label of the mainstream left, as that smear discredits instantly (although with diminishing effectiveness due to overuse). The reaction to traditional art is an aversion that smacks suspiciously of fear.

Revolutionaries challenge the dominant hegemony. Reactionaries perpetuate it. The artistic mainstream, preserved in the aspic of its century-old aesthetic and lavished with funds and commission from private foundations and government agencies, clearly fall into the latter category. But accusing another of that of which the accuser himself is guilty—"gaslighting"—is classic psychopathic behavior. This is not to brand all mainstream artists as psychopaths, but a certain paranoia cannot but underlie an establishment that so zealously labels those who question its orthodoxies as "reactionaries."

But what, after all, is wrong with this state of affairs? Should classical artists not, as the establishment would urge, "get with the times." As it turns out, the fixation of the artistic establishment in modernist aesthetics has led to a massive retreat of the fine arts from the public sphere. The public, increasingly mystified or even offended at the excesses of what is called high art, write it off as incomprehensible and retreat to the more familiar and comforting world of popular art.

Poetry once played a central role in public life; no major event occurred without a celebratory poem. The very office of poet laureate was created to satisfy the need for public poetry. Yes, the poet laureate was political, tasked with glorifying the king, but that a succession of kings saw a need to have their deeds glorified to the public through poetry testifies to the great value once placed on the art. And outside the royal court, poems were written for and recited at any public occasion. Poems were inscribed on monuments.

None of that happens anymore. Poetry has receded into the background, relegated only to the small circles of those who write it, and they write it primarily for each other. It becomes an echo chamber, detached from the wider world and wielding no influence there. The same can be said of all other fine arts. The utter esotericism of contemporary styles leave only its most fervid devotees interested in it, and venues to showcase it little more than vanity projects to allow for mutual preening among elite circles.

And as the public retreats from the fine arts, its gravitation towards popular art coarsens the culture. Popular art, consciously or not, imitates high art. Thus, it comes as no surprise that the aesthetic pathologies plaguing high art have their parallels in popular art. High art became incomprehensible; popular art became crude. Both are nihilistic at their core.

A revival in an aesthetic of the fine arts that speaks to human imagination rather than cynical denial of reality, therefore, is necessary as a public service. In increasingly turbulent times, art will become necessary to reorient humanity towards meaning and towards the good that must exist in opposition to so much evil.

Thus, the arts—all arts: painting, sculpture, architecture, poetry, music—need a secession. "Secession," of course, to American ears resounds with the echo of the Confederacy, and is therefore tinged with the air of reaction. But artists, even in the United States, should not shy away from the term. If anything, its connotation with the events of 1860-61 are wonderfully attention-grabbing, and a marvelous way to troll the morally preening.

An artistic secession has nothing to do with armies, or with America, for that matter. It is an artistic term with a storied history. Several artistic secessions have sought to elevate artistic standards and freedom. The first such secession was the 1890 Salon du Champs-de-Mars, founded by the painter Pierre Puvis de Chavannes and the sculptor Auguste Rodin as a rebellion against what they saw as declining standards in the visual arts. Secession movements caught on, particularly in the German-speaking world. The Munich Secession of 1892 and the Berlin Secession of 1898 formed to operate free from establishment oversight. But most famous was the Vienna Secession of 1897, led by Gustav Klimt, which sought to achieve a "total art" that combined painting, architecture, and the decorative arts. This group included the painters Alphonse Mucha and Max Kurzweil, the architects Josef Hoffmann, Otto Wagner, and Joseph Maria Olbrich, and the designer Koloman Moser. Of a slightly different stripe was the Dresden Secession of 1919, which was an Expressionist reaction to the turmoil following World War I.

The time has come for artists—poets included—to build on this tradition. What, though, does a present-day artistic secession look like? In fact, it resembles very much a political secession.

First and foremost, its members must forswear any participation in or glorification of establishment honors. What commands the adulation of the establishment, especially the establishment media, they must hold in contempt. Nobel and Pulitzer Prizes, Guggenheim and MacArthur Fellowships, Academy and Tony Awards, laureateships, endowed chairs—these must no longer be mentioned with any air of awe or praise. These are nothing more than the stamp of approval of a cultural mainstream that has unquestioningly accepted—and in most cases fostered—the degradation of the fine arts. Far from advocating for high artistic standards, these awards and positions have become indicators of cultural degeneracy to the point where they can no longer be taken seriously by artists with high aesthetic standards. They have become contemptible, and should merit the contempt of serious artists.

Second, the secession must set up its own parallel structures: publishers for poets, authors, and composers (self-publishing is not enough; our publishing must be free from the whims of Amazon); galleries for the visual arts; concert venues and ensembles for musicians; theaters and troupes for actors; studios for filmmakers. All of these organizations must be allied. The establishment will ignore them at first, but any degree of success will draw an attack. Strength lies in unity and numbers; only a united form will withstand the full fury of establishment wrath.

These organization should cultivate a parallel system of awards and honors—secession equivalents for the Pulitzer Prizes and the poet laureateships. Monetary prizes, grants, and scholarships should also advance poets, artists, and composers working in a traditional aesthetic. Funding is the lifeblood of any organized effort and will be key to establishing a parallel system of venues and prizes.

And finally, and most basically, individual creators—poets, authors, artists, composers, performers—should work together in mutual support. Minor differences in artistic visions, political ideologies, and individual styles, as well as basic personality conflicts are only natural and are bound to occur. Seceding artists must navigate these as in all human relationships, but they must never let them interfere with either the vision or mission of the secession. Without a united front and a network of mutual friendship and both moral and financial support, there is no movement, and any effort by individuals in its direction will be doomed. Remember the leviathan of entrenched, well-financed, mass media-supported interests arrayed ready to crush any opposition to the official narrative. An individual confronting it can hope only for martyrdom; a united front alone can achieve victory.

Great things have small beginnings, and every one of the most prestigious establishment awards once started as a first-time experiment, without the dust of age or the halo of prestige to distinguish it. So this movement must start, but with dedication and perseverance it, too, will one day achieve a level of prestige on par with establishment awards. Indeed, they may one day supplant the establishment altogether.

If we, not just classical poets, but all artists who work in a traditional aesthetic, truly believe in our ideals, we must put our beliefs into action, stand up for our ideals and against those who despise them, and—most importantly—be willing to sacrifice acceptance of the mainstream to build something. The artistic mainstream—as with the political and academic mainstream—is utterly bankrupt. What satisfaction could any serious artist have from its acceptance? None. Our solution is to build—to create where our detractors would only destroy. So let us build!

Poets

Anderson, C.B. was the longtime gardener for the PBS television series *The Victory Garden*. Hundreds of his poems have appeared in scores of print and electronic journals out of North America, Great Britain, Ireland, Austria, Australia, and India. His collection *Mortal Soup and the Blue Yonder* was published in 2013 by White Violet Press and his newest collection *Roots in the Sky, Boots on the Ground* was published by Kelsay Books in 2019.

Anthony, K.S. is an NYC-based writer and occasional marketing executive. His website is ksanthony.net

Arredondo, Anna J. is a Pennsylvania native now residing in Colorado. She is an engineer by education, a home educator by choice, and by preference, a poet.

Benson Brown, Andrew has had poems and reviews published in a few journals. His epic-in-progress, *Legends of Liberty*, will chronicle the major events of the American Revolution if he lives to complete it. Though he writes history articles for *American Essence* magazine, he lists his primary occupation on official forms as "poet." He is, in other words, a vagabond.

Bonham, Warren is a private equity investor who lives in Southlake, Texas

Bryant, Mike is a poet and retired plumber living on the Gulf Coast of Texas. He is the Moderator for the Society of Classical Poets website.

Bryant, Susan Jarvis is the winner of the 2020 International SCP Poetry Competition, and has been nominated for the 2022 Pushcart Prize.

Buchheit, Paul is an author of books, poems, progressive essays, and scientific journal articles. He recently completed his first historical novel, *1871: Rivers on Fire*.

Canerdy, Janice is a retired high-school English teacher from Potts Camp, Mississippi. Her first book, *Expressions of Faith* (Christian Faith Publishing), was published in December 2016.

Casey, Aidan was born in Dublin, Ireland and studied English and Philosophy at University College Dublin. Since then, he has taught English in Spain and Germany, where he now lives.

Coats, Margaret lives in California. She holds a Ph.D. in English and American literature and language from Harvard University. She has retired from a career of teaching literature, languages, and writing that included considerable work in home-schooling for her own family and others.

Cook, Sally is both a poet and a painter residing in upstate New York. A six-time nominee for a Pushcart award. She has received several awards from the World Order of Narrative and Formalist Poets. She is winner of the 2022 SCP International Poetry Competition.

Cooper, Monika is an American family woman.

Corey, Cheryl is a Connecticut poet. She is also an author of short stories, a novella, and recently completed a novel.

Crozier, Patricia Rogers holds a B.S. in Physics from Mississippi College. She resides in Gulf Breeze, Florida, where she works at the bakery in Publix.

DesBois, Jack is a singer, actor, and storyteller. He gives annual Epiphany season performances of *The Western Star*, which he wrote in 2016. He self-published a chapbook of short poems in 2018. As a singer, Jack has had the good fortune to solo in several of the great works of Baroque Oratorio, including Handel's Messiah (Bass) and Esther (Haman) and J.S. Bach's St. John Passion (Jesus). Jack lives in Topsfield, Massachusetts.

Dickey, Stephen M. is a Slavic linguist at the University of Kansas. He has published widely on Slavic verbal categories, and has published translations of Bosnian, Croatian, and Serbian fiction and poetry including Meša Selimović's *Death and the Dervish*, Borislav Pekić's *How to Quiet a Vampire*, and Miljenko Jergović's *Ruta Tannenbaum*.

Donovan, Johanna is a transplanted Swiss now growing in New England who gets up to write.

Duncan, Shaun C. is a picture framer and fine art printer who lives in Adelaide, South Australia.

Eardley, Jeff lives in the heart of England near to the Peak District National Park and is a local musician who plays guitar, mandolin, and piano steeped in the music of America.

Erlandson, Cynthia is a poet and fitness professional living in Michigan. Her second collection of poems, *Notes on Time*, has recently been published by AuthorHouse, as was her first (2005) collection, *These Holy Mysteries*.

Erlandson, Paul resides in Royal Oak Michigan, and has recently retired from an automotive engineering career with Ford Motor Company.

Essmann, Jeffrey is an essayist and poet living in New York. His poetry has appeared in numerous magazines and literary journals and various venues of the Benedictine monastery with which he is an oblate. He is editor of the Catholic Poetry Room page on the Integrated Catholic Life website.

Fillion, Adrian, a retired proofreader, lives in Lawrenceville, Georgia. He won the 2018 Ron Boggs Memorial Poetry Contest, hosted by the Johns Creek Poetry Group in Johns Creek, Georgia. Several of his poems have appeared in small, local publications.

Frank, Joshua C. works in the field of statistics and lives near Austin, Texas.

Freeman, Paul A. is the author of *Rumours of Ophir*, a crime novel that was taught in Zimbabwean high schools and has been translated into German. In addition to having two novels, a children's book, and an 18,000-word narrative poem (*Robin Hood and Friar Tuck: Zombie Killers!*) commercially published, Paul is the author of hundreds of published short stories, poems, and articles.

Gardner, Mary is a poet living in Florida.

Grein, Dusty is a poet, novelist, editor, and book producer. His written work has been published in numerous magazines and books, as well as in print and online journals. He has had poetry translated into several languages worldwide, is the co-author of a book on crafting classical poetry, and his How To articles can be found reprinted in several locations. Dusty lives, works, and plays in the Pacific Northwestern United States. There he enjoys spending his time, whenever possible, spoiling many of his twenty-one grandchildren before sending them back home to their parents.

Haase, Lucia has several books of poetry published. She lives in Spring Valley, Illinois.

Harrison, Maura H. is a poetry student in the Master of Fine Arts in Creative Writing program at the University of St. Thomas. She lives in Fredericksburg, Virginia.

Hook, Talbot is a PhD student and occasional writer currently living in Connecticut.

Horne, Kenneth L. is an emerging poet in Colorado.

Howard, Daniel Joseph studied law in his native Ireland before taking his MA in philosophy at King's College London. After working in the European Commission, he is now pursuing a PhD in Philosophy at Boston College.

James, Leland is the author of five poetry collections, four children's books in verse, and a book on creative writing and poetry craft. He has published over three hundred poems worldwide He was the winner of the Aesthetica Creative Writing Award and has won or received honors in many other competitions, both in the USA and Europe. Leland has been featured in American Life in Poetry and was recently nominated for a Pushcart Prize. (Lelandjamespoet.com)

Kay, Pippa lives in Sydney Australia. She has had three books published: *Doubt & Conviction: The Kalajzich Inquiry* (non-fiction, 2001), *Back Stories* (collected stories, 2002) and *Keeping it in the Family* (collected stories, 2018). Keeping it in the Family won the Society of Women Writers Fiction Prize in 2018. Her website is Pippakay.com.au.

Kemper, Jeff has been a biology teacher, biblical studies instructor, editor, and painting contractor. He lives in York County, Pennsylvania.

Kidd, Joe is a working, published poet and songwriter, touring North America and Western Europe. In 2020, he published *The Invisible Waterhole*, a collection of spiritual and sensual verse. He has been awarded by the Michigan Governor's Office and the U.S. House of Representatives for his work to advance Peace and Social Justice. Joe is a member of National & International Beat Poet Foundation (USA), Angora Poets (Paris France), the Society of Classical Poets, and 100,000 Poets For Change International. He has been appointed Official Beat Poet Laureate of the State of Michigan 2022-2024.

Kinsky, Carl is a country lawyer living in Ste. Genevieve, Missouri.

Kotsybar, James Ph. is a poet and owner of Chaotic Exotics orchid nursery, in California.

Lee, Catherine, originally from New Zealand, is an expatriate currently residing in Thailand. Previously a Purchasing Agent in the hospitality industry, she is now a freelance professional proofreader and editor. In Australia, she has been the recipient of such prizes as the Blackened Billy Award, Ipswich International Prize, Bryan Kelleher Literary Award, Henry Lawson Society Award, and others. She is a member of several poetry associations, and host editor of the Poets Birthdays and Poets of Yesteryear pages for the monthly Australian magazine, *FreeXpresSion*.

Lillios, Peter resides in Sound Beach, New York. He is an auditor by profession.

Lott, Rachel A. holds a PhD in medieval philosophy from the University of Toronto. Her first volume of translations, *The Sorcerers' Stone: Alchemical Poems* by Angelus Silesius, was published in 2023.

Johnson, Jeremiah received his MA in Rhetoric in 2003 and then ran off to China to teach for a decade. He is also currently a teacher of English Composition and World Literature at the University of North Georgia. He lives in Cumming, GA.

Magdalen, Daniel is a doctoral student in the Faculty of Letters at the University of Bucharest, in Romania.

Maibach, Michael Charles began writing poems at age 9. Since then, he has continued writing poems and sharing them with friends. His career has involved global business diplomacy. He is a native of Peoria, Illinois. Today Michael resides in Old Town Alexandria, Virginia. His poems can be viewed at MaibachPoems.us

Mantyk, Evan teaches history and literature in the Hudson Valley region of New York. He is president of the Society of Classical Poets, as well as chief editor of its website and Journal. His most recent book of poetry, *Heroes of the East and West*, was published in 2020.

Mootsey, Bethany is a stay-at-home mom and foster mom living in Clearwater, Florida. She is a Covenant College graduate with publications in "Church Educator."

Myers, Mary Jane resides in Springfield, Illinois. She is a retired JD/CPA tax specialist. Her debut short story collection *Curious Affairs* was published by Paul Dry Books in 2018.

Handley-Schachler, Morrison is a retired Chartered Public Finance Accountant and Lecturer in Accounting. He has a doctorate in Ancient History and has published articles on ancient Persian history, accounting history, financial crime, auditing and financial risk management. He lives in South Queensferry, on the outskirts of Edinburgh, Scotland.

Naegele, Gail Kaye is a poet who has worked as a nurse.

Pain, Norma was born in Liverpool, England and now lives in Parksville, British Columbia, Canada. She was twice nominated for the Pushcart Prize. She self-published a book of rhyme in 2000 called *Bulging Assets*.

Peterson, LTC Roy E. is a U.S. Army Military Intelligence and Russian Foreign Area Officer (Retired) who has published more than 5,000 poems in 78 of his 101 books. He has been an Army Attaché in Moscow, Commander of INF Portal Monitoring in Votkinsk, first U.S. Foreign Commercial Officer in Vladivostok, Russia and Regional Manager in the Russian Far East for IBM. He has taught at the University of Arizona, Western New Mexico University, University of Maryland, Travel University and the University of Phoenix.

Pietrack, Michael is a writer, businessman, and former baseball player who resides in Colorado. Earlier this year his book *Legacy: The Saga Begins*, a 14-chapter narrative poem, was published.

Rhodes, Royal is a retired professor of global religions at Kenyon College, and a life-long student of the Classics. He studied under the late Robert Fisher Healey S.J., Oxford and Harvard educated authority on ancient literature and the co-author of the important edition of the *Sacred Calendar of Eleusis*.

Rizley, Martin grew up in Oklahoma and in Texas, and has served in pastoral ministry both in the United States and in Europe. He is currently serving as the pastor of a small evangelical church in the city of Málaga on the southern coast of Spain.

Robin, Damian lives in England, where he works as a copyeditor and proofreader. He lives with his wife and two of their three adult children. He won Second Place in the Society's 2014 Poetry Competition.

Rogers, Phil S. is a sixth generation Vermonter, age 72, now retired and living in Texas. He served in the U.S. Air Force and had a career in real estate and banking. He previously published *Everlasting Glory*, a historical work.

Sale, James has had over 50 books published, most recently, "Mapping Motivation for Top Performing Teams" (Routledge, 2021). He has been nominated by *The Hong Kong Review* for the 2022 Pushcart Prize for poetry, has won first prize in The Society of Classical Poets 2017 annual competition, and performed in New York in 2019. He is a regular contributor to *The Epoch Times*. His most recent poetry collections are *HellWard* and *StairWell* (the first two parts in a three-part epic). For more information about the author, and about his Dante project, visit englishcantos.home.blog

Salemi, Joseph S. has published five books of poetry, and his poems, translations, and scholarly articles have appeared in over one hundred publications worldwide. He is the editor of the literary magazine *Trinacria*. He teaches in the Department of Humanities at New York University and in the Department of Classical Languages at Hunter College.

Sarangi, Satyananda is a young civil servant by profession and an electrical engineering alumnus of Indira Gandhi Institute of Technology. Currently, he resides in Odisha, India.

Scheltens, Isabel teaches at a Lutheran Classical school in Fort Wayne, Indiana, where she shares a love of history, literature, and music with her students.

Sedia, Adam (b. 1984) lives in his native Northwest Indiana where he practices law as a civil and appellate litigator. He is also a composer, and his musical works may be heard on his YouTube channel.

Shrayer, Maxim D. is an author and a professor at Boston College. His recent books include *Of Politics and Pandemics*, a collection of English-language verse, and *Stikhi iz aipada*, a collection of Russian-language verse. Shrayer's new memoir, *Immigrant Baggage*, is forthcoming in 2023.

Smagacz, Geoffrey writes from South Carolina and Mexico. A collection of his fiction, titled *A Waste of Shame and Other Sad Tales of the Appalachian Foothills* (Wiseblood Books, 2013), won the 2014 Independent Publisher gold medal for Best Mid-Atlantic Regional Fiction.

Southerland, Charles is a farmer who writes poetry and short stories. He also makes and sells walking sticks, canes and shillelaghs. He is American by birth and Scottish by heritage. He can trace his recent roots to the 1600s in Dunfermline and Torryburn in County Fife, Scotland.

Stone, Mark F. worked as an attorney for the United States Air Force for 33 years. He is a retired Lieutenant Colonel. He began writing poems in 2005, as a way to woo his bride-to-be into wedlock. Some of his poems and photographs can be found at: markfstone.substack.com. He grew near Seattle and now lives in Ohio.

Stuart, Joseph is a lawyer living and practicing in Northern Virginia. He maintains the blog Mightyinditers.typepad.com/hereunder/

Thomas, Christiana is a homeschooled 12th grade student in Oregon.

Todd, S.A. lives in the Northeast of England. A volume of his collected works, *Deeds And Abstracts—A Poetry Collection*, is available on Amazon.

Tuton, Dan is a poet living in Albuquerque, New Mexico. After an initial career as a family therapist, he has been ordained as an Episcopal priest since early in 2004. He initially served a parish in the Baltimore area for four years, and have been the Vicar, then Rector of Hope in the Desert in Albuquerque since 2007.

Tweedie, James A. is a retired pastor living in Long Beach, Washington. He has written and self-published four novels and a collection of short stories. He won the 2021 SCP International Poetry Competition.

Valle, Cara is an English teacher and Catholic homeschooling mother, living in Virginia.

Villanueva, Angel L. is a poet residing in Massachusetts.

Wasem, Adam is a writer living in Utah.

Watt, David is a writer from Canberra, the "Bush Capital" of Australia who works for IP (Intellectual Property) Australia. He has contributed regularly to *Collections of Poetry and Prose* by Robin Barratt.

Watts, Anthony has been writing *seriously* for about 50 years. He has won 26 First Prizes in poetry competitions and was longlisted for the National Poetry Competition 2014. His poems have appeared in many magazines and anthologies. His fifth collection, *Stiles*, is published by Paekakariki Press. A retired library assistant, his home is in rural Somerset (United Kingdom).

Whidden, Phillip is an American living in England who has been published in America, England, Scotland (and elsewhere) in book form, online, and in journals.

Whippman, David is a British poet, now retired after a career in healthcare. Over the years he's had quite a few poems, articles, and short stories published in various magazines.

Willis, Lionel was born in Toronto in 1932. He has been a mosaic designer, portrait painter, watercolorist, biological illustrator, field entomologist and professor of English Literature as well as a poet. His verse has appeared in two books, *The Dreamstone and Other Rhymes* (The Plowman, 2003) and *Heartscape, a Book of Bucolic Verse* (EIDOLON, 2019).

Winick, Russel started writing poetry at nearly age 65, after ending a long legal career. He resides in Naperville, Illinois.

Wirkala, Elwin was in the Peace Corps in his early twenties and subsequently spent two plus decades in South America, gaining near native fluency in Portuguese and Spanish. He has translated Sor Juana Inés de la Cruz's sonnets and the great *Primer Sueño*, on which he is writing a book.

Woodruff, Julian D. was a teacher, orchestral musician, and librarian. He served for several years as librarian at the Crocker Art Museum in Sacramento, California. He now resides in the area of Rochester, New York, where he writes poetry and fiction, much of it for children.

Yapko, Brian is a lawyer who also writes poetry. He lives in Santa Fe, New Mexico.

HONY SOYT QUI MAL PENCE
Shame on anyone who thinks evil of it.

Printed in the USA
CPSIA information can be obtained
at www.ICGtesting.com
LVHW011909300823
756644LV00001B/2